adored

by the God
who sees me

Kerry Clarensau *and* Kay Burnett

GPH®
Gospel Publishing House

The Scripture reference is given for each Bible woman's story.
To put their stories in narrative form, names, dialogue, and events have
been added to fill out elements not given in the Scripture text.

Names have been changed in instances where it has been necessary to
protect the privacy of the individuals mentioned.

02-4112
ISBN: 978-1-60731-570-4

Printed in the United States of America

21 20 19 18 • 1 2 3 4

Dedication

I dedicate this book to our girls—Katie, Molly, Lennon, Danielle, and Winnie. When Mike and I were first married, I prayed for four children. At the age of twenty-one, having two boys and then two girls seemed like the ideal family. Our son Tyler was born just months after our first anniversary; and Blake was on his way the moment we were ready for a second child. We soon had two sons, just like we had prayed. We were ready for our girls, but I couldn't become pregnant again. To be honest, I experienced intense moments of disappointment. Our family felt incomplete. Then God answered our prayers in the most surprising way! He gave us two amazing daughters-in-law. I couldn't love them any more if I had given birth to them. They complete that generation perfectly—two boys and two girls. Next came the sweetest blessings we've experienced thus far: three precious granddaughters! I pray for each of our girls to understand how much God truly adores them. May they trust His extravagant love and rest in the knowledge that He sees them intimately. With His watchful eye, He will redeem them, guide them, and provide exactly what is needed every moment of their journey. May the pages of this book inspire them to embrace a relationship with Him in ever-increasing ways.

—Kerry Clarensau

Dedication

I dedicate this book to all my girls: Leandra, Megan, Brynna, Aurora, Kayla, and Bexley. You bring inexpressible joy to my life. I love you and cherish every single one of you. Each of you is a priceless treasure in a unique and precious way. I'm a better person because of your influence in my life. My prayer is that you will know—truly know—just how important you are in God's plan. You have so much to offer to this broken and hurting world, as you press in deeper to knowing and loving God. Above even that, my heart's cry is for you to always know without a doubt, that your loving Heavenly Father sees you right where you are, in every difficult trial, in every season of struggle, failure, or pain, and through all the joyous, triumphant seasons as well. In the depths of God's heart, you are cherished, worthy, valued, beautiful, and loved. He sees you, my precious girls, and He adores you—and, I do too!

—Kay Burnett

Contents

Introduction **HAGAR**
The God Who Sees Me . . . . *Christy* 7

Chapter 1 **THE WOMAN AT THE WELL**
The God Who Sees My Deepest Needs . *Peggy* 15

Chapter 2 **MARY OF BETHANY**
The God Who Sees My Heart to Know Him. *Rachelle* 29

Chapter 3 **MARY MAGDALENE**
The God Who Sees My Brokenness . . *Hi'ilani* . .41

Chapter 4 **DEBORAH**
Challah
The God Who Sees My Place in His Work 55

Chapter 5 **HANNAH**
Karen
The God Who Sees My Deepest Longings 69

Chapter 6 **RUTH**
The God Who Sees My Destiny . . *Barbara* 83

Conclusion **THE WIDOW**
The God Who Sees Me Completely . . . *Pam* 97

Notes 102

About the Authors 103

Hagar—
The God Who Sees Me

Genesis 16

KAY BURNETT

Terrifying thoughts flooded her mind as she dropped to rest under an acacia tree. How had things become so desperate, so unbearable that she now found herself alone, running back to Egypt? Pregnant and left to the mercy of her mistress who had turned on her, Hagar had fled impulsively and now faced an impossible journey through a desert wilderness that stretched for miles before her. Overwhelmed by the challenge of it all, she wept.

⁕ She hadn't foreseen this unexpected change of events. She didn't mind serving her mistress, Sarai. Though the work was mundane at times, she found satisfaction in her duties and appreciated Sarai's kindness. Hagar's life in this new place with this wealthy couple had brought many advantages. She was grateful and relieved by this. But everything changed the day she was delivered to Abram as a surrogate wife, thrust into his arms through Sarai's desperate desire to provide her husband with an heir.

Certainly, she was thankful for the provisions and benefits that had come into her life through the master and his wife. Some time ago they had taken her and numerous other servants with them when they left Egypt. Since then, they had traveled, pitching their tents wherever Abram led them. At first, leaving Egypt had shaken Hagar, filling her with dread of the unknown. As one of the many servants and possessions Abram and Sarai had acquired while living in Egypt, she, along with others, now belonged to them and was forced to go wherever they went. Hagar had no choice but to accept this turn of fate and make the best of it. Though a woman in her lowly estate was usually treated more like a possession than a person, overall her master and mistress had been fair and kind to her. She always had plenty to eat, water to drink, and a safe place to live.

But once Hagar conceived Abram's child everything changed. Suddenly she knew she held a place her mistress couldn't hold in Abram's eyes—she was carrying his child. Her feelings toward her mistress gradually changed. Finally, for the first time in her life, she felt a little better than someone else, a little more favored, more blessed. Her behavior began to shift, starting in small and subtle ways but quickly growing bolder—a furtive look of disdain now and then, or a response with a superior air about it. Hagar became spiteful and insolent toward Sarai.

Pondering those choices and attitudes as she rested in the heat of the desert, Hagar realized she had been wrong—cruel even—to her mistress who, up until then, had worked her hard but had always been fair and provided for her needs.

So, it had come to this. Hagar sat in the shade of the acacia tree, tired, thirsty, and desperately fearful. Hot tears streamed down her face as she wrapped her arms around her growing belly. She had heard stories of people losing their lives in the brutal and unrelenting desert. Lack of water, venomous snakes, and unforeseen enemies had brought an end to many who traveled through this terrifying wilderness! Unsure of what to do, she rested beside a spring, where at least she had water. It might be the last she would find for quite some time. *Oh, what will become of me and my child who has begun to move in me?*

Suddenly, a movement nearby startled her. Terrified of being discovered, Hagar froze, striving to calm her sobs. Without warning, a figure appeared quietly before her. Unlike anything or anyone she had seen before, a man—no, an incredible being—drew near to her.

"Hagar, slave of Sarai, where have you come from, and where are you going?" (verse 8).

Heart pounding, she choked out the words, "I'm running away from my mistress Sarai" (verse 8) *Who is this person? Where did He come from? How does He know my name? Maybe He will help me.*

The kindness and strength in His eyes calmed her quaking heart and stirred her spirit deep within. Men typically didn't notice her, except for all the wrong reasons. Here stood a man who spoke to her with respect and concern. Yet, this was no ordinary man! Uncertain what to do or say, Hagar rose, shaking before this magnificent being. The power of His presence, the concern in His voice, and the gentleness of His approach calmed her heart and drew her into an immediate and profound trust.

His eyes pierced her soul. Again, He spoke, "Return to Sarai. Submit to her and settle into your place in her household. I'm going to multiply your descendants beyond any number you can count. The child you are carrying will be a son. You must call him

Ishmael, for I have seen your pain and suffering."

Hagar, encouraged by this message, declared, "You are the God who sees me!"

"The God who sees me." What a profound declaration!

Oh, how this hurting world needs someone to see them, notice them, and count them worthy of concern and love. The more we look with eyes to see, to really see the people around us, the more we realize they are aching and broken. Multitudes of beloved humanity made in the image of Almighty God exist all over the globe in a myriad physical and economic conditions. Some are hungry and sick, living in the severest poverty, uncertain whether they will have enough food or water to live another day. Others reside in multimillion-dollar mansions with every luxury and pleasure imaginable. Multitudes live between these two extremes, but all of us need more than mere physical sustenance, more than clothing and shelter.

Our soul, the miraculous eternal part of our being that distinguishes us from other creatures, has needs as well. Our souls hunger and thirst for meaning. Our souls long for the love of others from the time we draw our first breath. The soul is an artistic masterpiece from Father God who chose to imprint His image into humanity. Yet the heartaches and challenges of life can shatter the delicate, stained-glass beauty of our souls.

Questions and doubts about our value can speak so loudly inside our heads that we hear nothing else. Food can sustain the body and water can quench our physical thirst, but what will satisfy and soothe our aching, broken souls? Money can offer physical shelter and a tangible sense of security for the future. But what can riches do to heal the shattered soul of one who attains all the creature comforts this world offers yet finds herself cast aside and abandoned or ridiculed, her soul trampled and splintered into a million pieces?

Like Hagar, have you found yourself alone, confused, overwhelmed, and filled with despair? Perhaps, like Hagar, you're in the middle of a desert experience with no sign of help or hope, and your heart has reached a place beyond despair and discouragement.

Perhaps you're bearing the impact and burden of someone else's sin, and you feel confused about how to move forward. Has someone abandoned you and shredded any semblance of self-esteem and joy from your life? Are you unexpectedly alone and surrounded by responsibilities and commitments you have no idea how to fulfill?

Perhaps you're experiencing the pain of your own unfortunate choices. The compromises started out small but snowballed—now you feel hemmed in on every side by wrong decisions, unsure how to get your life back on track. Hope feels far away, and every moment reminds you of what you *don't* have, while you long for what you wish you *could* have.

Maybe you aren't in a hurtful situation or season at all. Perhaps you're pressing in to know God in deeper ways, studying His Word, and seeking to apply it. Somehow you still wonder at times if it all makes a difference. Does anyone see and care about your faithfulness? Others around you seem to be flourishing while you feel anonymous, overlooked, and neglected. You just wish someone, anyone, would notice you and engage you in a meaningful way.

We all have an inherent need to be valued. We all require

healing from the effects of our mistakes and the wounds this world and others have inflicted upon the treasure of our souls. We all need the touch and concern of others, but we have a deeper need for a love that surpasses what the world tries to offer.

Do you long for this? Do you sometimes feel as if no one could possibly know your longing to be seen and valued, to be treasured just for who you are, right in the middle of your messy circumstances?

I have great news for you! The infinite, all-knowing, all-powerful God who saw to the depths of Hagar's soul and intercepted her as she journeyed in the desert wants to do the same for you. This God—*your* God—sees you. He sees you right where you are. He sees where you've been and where you're going. He sees your mistakes and your successes. He sees your strengths and your weaknesses. He sees what you love and what you hate. He sees your heartbreak, your joy, and your triumph. He sees your deepest longings and knows exactly what you need. He sees it all—and He has more for you!

✳ God wants you to know that with perfect and eternal eyesight, *He sees you*. He yearns to comfort you, offer gentle correction, and point you in the right direction. This God who sees you wants to empower you for life's journey and show you the God-birthed and God-filled promises and plans He has for you. The life He offers is big and deep, filled with purpose and hope. He offers to guide you into all truth and put a firm foundation beneath your feet.

This God—this amazing-Creator-of-all-things God—wants you to know that He loves you. He treasures you and has incredible plans for you. I encourage you to let Him lead you in this journey. Though it may begin in a wilderness desert, you're certain to encounter mountain-top experiences that will exhilarate your soul. He wants your life to be stuffed full of joy and fulfillment. He has created assignments specifically for you—good things He planned before you even knew Him. Ephesians 2:10 says, "For we are his workmanship, created in Christ Jesus for good works, which God prepared beforehand, that we should walk in them" (ESV).

He has priceless promises in store for you and great purpose for your existence.

You, my friend, are loved.

You are longed for.

You are valued and cherished.

You are . . . *adored by the God who sees you.*

CHAPTER 1

The Woman at the Well—
The God Who Sees My Deepest Needs
John 4

KAY BURNETT

Sychar, Samaria—During Jesus' Ministry

The woman shifted the clay jar a bit to ease her tired arms. Powder-fine dust coated her feet and sandals as she walked beneath the heat of the noonday sun. Oh, how refreshing a hard rain would feel! Dalia kept her gaze on the path as she passed the village houses on her way to the well. By now, she knew what to expect, and she did what she could to minimize conversations with others.

Long ago she had given up the custom of gathering with the women of the village to draw water in the cooler hours of the day. When she was younger, she had enjoyed this daily encounter, sharing village news and hearing about the newest baby or betrothal. Friendships, as well as rivalries, were born at the well.

But through the years her status had shifted dramatically. Her offenses haunted her with waves of guilt and shame, especially when she walked through town. The villagers knew of her past as well as her current situation. Their whispers and disapproving looks stung like salt in a wound. To avoid others, she took a longer route or chose a less convenient time of day to draw water from Jacob's well.

The midday sun beat down on her as she slowly made her way to the well. The ache within her soul felt heavier than any physical burden she might carry. A few unwanted tears rose in her eyes, threatening to betray the thoughts she desperately wanted to hide. *Is this all there is to life? Is this life I'm trapped in all I was meant for?* From her earliest memory she had longed to be loved, valued, even cherished. She longed to feel safe and cared for, significant in someone's eyes.

Looking back on her past, she saw a series of relationships with men that had taken their toll, scarring her heart with each painful failure. Most recently, yearning once again for acceptance, she had stepped into a relationship without giving enough thought to the possible consequences. It was quickly becoming apparent that this relationship was yet another mistake. Sighing and willing the tears not to fall, she drew near to the well.

There, she noticed Someone resting nearby who was dusty and weary. She could tell from His appearance that He was a Jew. Dread flushed her face crimson. Focusing on her task, she hoped He wouldn't speak to her or accost her in any way. *Not today. Oh, please, just let me draw water and make it back home without any trouble.* She lowered her jar into the well.

His gaze took in her anxiety and agitation. Softly, He spoke. "Will you give me a drink?" (verse 7).

Was He speaking to her, asking her for water?

Years of unpleasant exchanges with Jews rose in her mind, fueling a quick and bitter response. "You are a Jew and I am a

Samaritan woman. How can you ask me for a drink?" (verse 9) Her jar reached the water and began to fill. He had no vessel to draw water, so she questioned His motives. She also knew too well how the Jews despised her people. In the eyes of a Jewish man there was no lower position than to be a Samaritan *and* a woman. Besides, it was forbidden for a Jew to drink from any vessel touched by a Samaritan woman, who was considered perpetually unclean.

Unfazed by her caustic response, Jesus said, "If you knew the gift of God and who it is that asks you for a drink, you would have asked him and he would have given you living water" (verse 10).

Flustered by this unexpected encounter with a stranger and caught off guard by His quiet manner, Dalia paused, studying Him as she drew the water jar up from the well. "Sir, you have nothing to draw with and the well is deep. Where can you get this living water? Are you greater than our father Jacob, who gave us the well and drank from it himself, as did also his sons and his livestock?" (verses 11 and 12).

His patience with her curt responses surprised her. He answered calmly, "Everyone who drinks this water will be thirsty again, but whoever drinks the water I give them will never thirst. Indeed, the water I give them will become in them a spring of water welling up to eternal life" (verses 13 and 14).

Something deep within her grasped that He was talking about more than water. Was there some kind of water that could quench her physical thirst and wash away more than the dust that coated her feet? Did He know of water that could wash away the shame that settled into every crack and crevice of a damaged heart?

This time, her reply came with a quiet longing instead of sarcasm. "Sir, please give me this water so that I'll never thirst again. Help me not to need to come here to draw water."

Please, she thought. *Help me. Fill this inner thirst that never goes away!*

Suddenly, without warning, emotions welled up within her and she responded to an inner thirst she had felt her entire life. Yes, she thirsted . . . thirsted for answers to lift her out of her lowly station in life, answers that would make it unnecessary to take this lonely walk to the well each day. *Yes!* She wanted to scream. *Yes! Give me living water! Give me what my soul is thirsting for, aching for.*

His gaze pierced her soul, seeming to look right into her wounded spirit. "Go bring your husband back here to the well."

Dropping her head, she spoke softly, remorse choking every word. "I have no husband." Shame enveloped her.

"That's right. In fact, you've had five husbands, and you're not married to the man you're with now."

How could He know about her? Expecting the customary disdain, she nervously raised her eyes to look at Him. What was this? She saw no condemnation in His gaze, but something else. He knew about her sin, yet His eyes still communicated personal dignity. Unlike everyone else who knew her past and present circumstances, this Man didn't look away or step back to distance Himself from her. He stated plainly what she, as well as others, knew—she was involved in a disgraceful and sordid lifestyle. Standing near Him, looking into His eyes, and hearing His quiet statement, she felt an acute awareness of her sin.

He was obviously a holy man—a prophet! Samaritans differed

from the Jews in their worship of God, blending pagan gods with the Jewish God. She never felt secure in the Samaritan way of worship. Questions she had harbored her entire life pushed to the surface.

"I know that Jews worship God only in Jerusalem. Our ancestors have always worshipped near this well, on this mountain." *Help me understand how to live, how to worship correctly! Maybe that is what is missing in my life.* Hadn't the Samaritan people been waiting and looking for the prophet who would follow Moses, bringing them restoration and hope?[1]

He responded kindly to her question. "There is a time coming when those who are true worshippers will worship the Father in spirit and in truth. For that is what the Father is looking for, those who will worship Him truly, from the depths of their hearts." He continued, "God is spirit, and His worshipers must worship in the Spirit and in truth."

Her heart was beating a little faster, and her spirit felt an uplifting tug. "Sir, it has been promised that the Messiah will come, and when He does, He will explain everything to us."

Jesus declared, "I, the one speaking to you—I am he" (verse 26).

This revelation stunned her. Instantly she believed He was the Christ. Leaving her water jar, Dalia ran back to the village. All her life she had searched for something or someone who could fill the void in her soul. She had longed for value and purpose. She had hungered for meaning and for truth. Her deep need for safety, companionship, and joy had driven her to the arms of men who could never fill the ache in her soul.

In a fleeting moment, her world shifted, taking her from spiritual and emotional despair to a revelation of truth, freedom, and joy. Immediately, the crushing weight of her spirit lifted, and for the first time in her life she felt free. She, a despised and sinful woman, had encountered the Christ—the Messiah! She felt clean, released from sin and shame. Where there had been pain and guilt, now flowed freedom and joy, hope and love. She had to tell others—anyone—everyone, about the One who was waiting at their well. The others must have the chance to meet Him, too!

An entire village heard about Jesus that day, and many, like Dalia, chose to follow Him.

Jesus defied the mores and culture of the day by speaking to a woman of despised origins and a disdained reputation. He demonstrated through His rule-shattering conversation with her that God valued her as much as the wealthy religious Jew named Nicodemus (see John 3:1–15). Status, reputation, or wealth didn't determine the value of a human soul in God's eyes.

Jesus saw a lost soul worth saving, and that is what He still sees today. Greek, Jew, Muslim, Hindu, male, female, old, or young, Jesus sees a priceless soul whom He cherishes and to whom He longs to bring redemption and freedom. Jesus is still seeking the hurting and lost; and there are many versions of Dalia's story in our world today.

Jesus was revolutionary in His days on this Earth. He never bowed to convention or ungodly cultural norms. He chose to travel through Samaria that day. He could have chosen a different route to avoid the Samaritan village, but He chose to journey through it instead. Jesus also chose to speak to this woman—a Samaritan *and* a woman. A rabbi would never converse openly with a woman, especially a Samaritan woman who was known as sinful and considered unclean. Yet Jesus chose to reach out to her.

Everything Jesus said and did while on Earth was purposeful, loving, and truthful. This is evident in His encounter with the Samaritan woman. He connected her physical need for water to her spiritual need for the only thing that could satisfy the longings of her heart—the Living Water that only He could offer. He used His prophetic revelation about her past and present relationships not to condemn her and make her feel guilty and shamed, but to open her heart to the truth, leading to the answer she needed—redemption.

A Twenty-First Century Story

As a Jewish rabbi, Jesus' decision to speak to a Samaritan woman was unexpected. It opened the door to her redemption and to salvation for many others in her village. Through His compassionate heart, He continues to pursue the lost today, as we see in the story of my friend Jackie.

Jackie captured my heart the instant I shook her hand. With her trendy asymmetrical hairstyle and crazy-print Capri pants, at ninety years of age she made quite a statement. Her spunky, fun appearance screamed, *I'm an interesting character. You should get to know me.* Her smile and warmth gave no hint of a life story that included years of pain and life-altering mistakes.

We chatted in a quiet corner, savoring our cookies and tea. She dove right into conversation, asking me questions about my life and my family, putting me at ease and somehow making me feel important. When I asked about her life, she shared her story with surprising transparency.

In the 1940s, as a wife and a mother of four, Jackie relished her sweet life. She had what most women wanted: a husband she loved, children she adored, and a comfortable lifestyle. But her world came crashing down the day her husband abandoned her and their children for his secretary. Jackie never saw it coming. The shock knocked the breath out of her. The suddenness of the betrayal, along with her years as a stay-at-home mom, placed her and the children in a vulnerable financial position.

Desperate to find a way to support herself and her children, she immediately accepted an entry-level job and tried as best she could to move forward. Her heart was shattered not only for her lost marriage but for the many ways her precious children would suffer. She felt utterly worthless and struggled with the cultural prejudices of the day. Jackie shared how people in that era thought, *You aren't much of a woman if you can't keep your man happy.*

Maneuvering through day-to-day life in all the familiar places was painful. Jackie heard the whispers and noticed the demeaning glances as she struggled to care for her children without falling apart. *Maybe it was true,* she thought. *Maybe I don't measure up. Maybe I wasn't good enough to make my husband happy, to keep him out of the arms of another woman.* Knowing it was impossible to go back and try again, Jackie slid into a deep, dark emotional hole.

A brief time later a man came into her life, bringing attention and plenty of compliments. He was thoughtful and interested in her, and he listened to her story with a compassionate heart. He made her feel not only better, but beautiful again—desired and valued, somehow. Oh, how his attention soaked deep into her wounded soul!

Blindsided by her emotions, Jackie quickly tumbled into his arms, hungry for someone to love her unconditionally and truly value her. Shaken and terrified when she learned she was pregnant, Jackie poured out the news to him, unsure how he would respond. He also proved to be less than honorable when he, too, abandoned her and their unborn child.

Her life had been damaged and shaky before, but what would others think of her now? Pregnant, unmarried, and abandoned once again, Jackie hit rock-bottom in that dark and dreadful season. Knowing her children had to come first, she moved forward as best she could, working low-paying jobs and struggling to raise five children alone while searching for meaning and healing in her life.

Thankfully, her story didn't end there. Jackie met Jesus and began a new life of healing and transformation. Thrilled and thankful for salvation and the promise of eternity with God, she served Christ wholeheartedly. Jesus filled her aching heart and met her lifelong need for acceptance and purpose.

Jackie found a place of belonging in the church she attended. Surrounded by a spiritual family who adored her and enjoyed her company, she grew deeper in her relationship with the Lord and freer through His healing power.

* * *

Jackie finished sharing her story with me, and we both dabbed at our tears. Then she added, "Last night, hearing the message the speaker shared impacted my heart like never before. For the first time since those painful early days, I feel the shame lifted off me. The heavy weight of guilt is gone. I feel free!" Her face radiated true freedom.

Jackie had received a beautiful gift from God through a simple message at a women's event. Jesus is still showing up at the well!

I could have jumped out of my seat in utter joy for her freedom, but my heart also ached at the thought that for the past fifty years Jackie had carried some shame for her past sins and mistakes. She loved Jesus and had accepted His gift of salvation. She enjoyed His ongoing presence in her life. She had lived these past decades serving Him faithfully and loving others. Yet in all those years she had not known total freedom from her painful past. She had continued to see herself through tainted lenses that labeled her a failure. Jesus never intended for her to carry such shame for fifty years.

Praise God, He can work in our lives in every single season of life, even when we're nearing one hundred years old. No matter who we are, God can meet our needs. He can make His Word come alive in our hearts and set us free from failure and regrets!

What about you, friend?

The Samaritan woman had a natural need to be loved and valued, and in her younger years she had sought to fill that need, as Jackie had, through painful relationships. Our human need to be loved and valued must be met at its deepest place by God alone. Then, when human relationships fail or people betray us, our value as a person isn't damaged or destroyed. When we place our value in God, we can weather the storms and painful seasons of life.

Both the Samaritan woman and Jackie searched for water to quench a spiritual thirst that people couldn't fulfill. They tried to fill their souls by "drinking water" from human sources through relationships that couldn't satisfy and ultimately failed. Jesus saw the Samaritan woman at the well that day, truly *saw* her. He understood her deepest need to be loved and valued. He had valued her before she drew her first breath. Jesus also saw Jackie suffering through the heartbreaking betrayal by men in her life. He saw her tumble into sin out of her deepest need to be loved and valued. He saw every tear she cried, every attempt to find the answers for her broken heart in all the wrong places. He saw both women when others overlooked them or mistreated them, and He loved them.

What well are you drinking from that isn't satisfying you? What are you filling up on that comes from a human source instead of the living Christ? Are you aching inside because of a longing you don't know how to fill?

Are you struggling over past rejections, past sins and failures, buried by a heavy weight of shame? Have others wrongly shaped your life through hurtful words? Perhaps you haven't relied on relationships for your value but on achievements, titles, or possessions.

In truth, our deepest need to be known, loved, and valued can only be met through a relationship with Jesus. He alone has the power to forgive our sins and mend our souls. Only He can offer a life free from guilt and shame. You don't have to be held back or live heavyhearted today because of mistakes you made yesterday. Jesus doesn't want you to live one single hour in bondage to shame! He wants you to receive His love and forgiveness.

He sees you, dear one. He sees your deepest needs as no one else can. He sees you, He loves you, and He values you. He wants to fulfill the needs of your life as nothing and no one else can.

He is your answer and He fulfills your identity if you accept the love He offers.

He sees you, and . . . He *adores* you.

Let's consider how God sees our deepest needs:

- Only God can meet our deepest need to be loved and valued.

- God looks beyond our sins and failures to the person He created us to be.

- God can use our story to bring salvation, encouragement, and freedom to others.

- As Christians, God calls us to walk in freedom, not bound by guilt and shame.

THINGS TO CONSIDER

1. What "well" do you turn to instead of turning to God for fulfillment, peace, and comfort?

2. Ask the Holy Spirit to reveal to you anyone you haven't fully forgiven. Consider writing in your prayer journal a statement of forgiveness to the people God brings to mind.

3. If you still carry guilt and shame from past mistakes, consider writing some of the verses listed in this book on index cards. Read them numerous times each day. Tape them to your mirror, carry them in your purse, or commit them to memory. Let the Word of God wash your heart and mind with His loving forgiveness and fill you with truth.

Scriptures to satisfy your soul

I will be fully satisfied as with the richest of foods;
with singing lips my mouth will praise You.

~PSALM 63:5

The LORD will guide you always; he will satisfy your needs in a
sun-scorched land and will strengthen your frame. You will be like
a well-watered garden, like a spring whose waters never fail.

~ISAIAH 58:11

"Blessed are those who hunger and thirst for righteousness,
for they will be filled."

~MATTHEW 5:6

Let them give thanks to the LORD for his unfailing love
and his wonderful deeds for mankind, for he satisfies the
thirsty and fills the hungry with good things.

~PSALM 107:8–9

The LORD is close to the brokenhearted and saves those
who are crushed in spirit.

~PSALM 34:18

"Eye has not seen, nor ear heard, nor have entered into the heart of
man the things which God has prepared for those who love Him."

~1 CORINTHIANS 2:9, NKJV

If we confess our sins, he is faithful and just and will forgive
us our sins and purify us from all unrighteousness.

~1 JOHN 1:9

APPLICATION/DISCUSSION QUESTIONS

1. Do you know a woman who was looking to other sources to meet her needs and then encountered Jesus? How did Jesus address her needs?

2. Name some common sources women may turn to in place of God as they look for meaning, significance, and fulfillment.

3. How do women act in unhealthy ways with one another? What alternate behaviors would honor God and each other?

4. How might God use our testimonies to draw others to Himself?

5. Take a few minutes to share an example of how God has met your deepest needs.

Journal prompt

Write a few sentences to describe the deepest needs in your life. Ask the Holy Spirit to reveal any ways you might be substituting ungodly sources for answers to those needs. Ask Him to show you how the presence of God and His Word can fulfill your needs.

CHAPTER 2

Mary of Bethany—
The God Who Sees My Heart to Know Him

Luke 10:38–42; John 11–12:8

KERRY CLARENSAU

Bethany—During Jesus' Ministry

Martha's home brimmed with life. The aroma of delicious food permeated the air, making stomachs growl in expectation. Hungry, travel-weary men gathered in the main room of the home. Some sat on couches and makeshift chairs; others sat on the floor or leaned against the wall—her guests filled every corner of the room. They were happy to be indoors, out of the sun and wind. Conversations hummed around the house as her visitors shared vivid descriptions of the amazing week they had spent with Jesus. While their faces exposed a measure of exhaustion, the excitement was unmistakable as they chatted with each other.

Meanwhile, Martha bustled around the house making sure the tables were set just right. She cleaned last-minute messes from the meal preparation. She adjusted the pots over the coals,

ensuring each dish was done to perfection. After all, she needed
to uphold her reputation as one of Bethany's best cooks. Martha
loved the details of hospitality and housekeeping, and she was
good at them, but, unfortunately, as a result she noticed every
crumb and speck of dust on the floor. She grabbed a broom, put
it in her sister's hand and motioned for her to get busy sweeping the floors. Martha was so busy making sure everything was
perfect for the meal, she barely heard a word her guests shared.

Mary obediently took the broom and began to sweep the
floor, but she was so drawn to what Jesus was saying that her
heart wasn't in her task. She knew too well that the places around
great teachers like Jesus were usually reserved for men. Yet despite time-honored traditions, Mary felt He welcomed her to join
those listening to His teaching. *Maybe I can sweep and still hear
what Jesus is saying if I move just a little closer.* As she inched her
way toward Jesus, her sweeping motions slowed, and it wasn't
long before the broom leaned motionless against the doorframe.
Mary found a spot to sit on the floor in front of Jesus—captivated
by His every word.

Drawn to the ideas He shared, nothing else mattered in that
moment but the life-giving Words from His heart. He was unlike
anyone else she knew. Everything He said seemed to penetrate
her soul in an indescribable way. His words brought conviction,
yet also hope and peace. *Oh, how I want to linger in His presence.*
Mary silently prayed she would be able to retain and understand
everything He said.

Lost in Jesus' words, Mary wasn't aware that Martha was vis-
ibly irritated with her. Martha subtly coughed and tried to draw
Mary's attention back to the broom, but Mary didn't take her

eyes off Jesus. So, Martha picked up the broom, walked behind Jesus, and looked right at Mary. She began sweeping the floor with exaggerated motions. "Surely, Mary will notice now and get up to help me," Martha murmured. A few of Jesus' friends had to hide their laughter as they noticed Martha's antics. But her sister sat perfectly still, oblivious to anything but what Jesus was saying. Finally, Martha couldn't take it for another moment and in complete frustration she blurted out, "Seriously! Jesus, don't you care that I'm doing all this work by myself? Tell my sister to get up and help me!" (author's paraphrase of Luke 10:40).

Maybe more was going on in Martha's heart than simple irritation at doing the domestic chores by herself. Was she upset that Mary was assuming the posture of a disciple by sitting and listening to Jesus' teaching? Perhaps Martha also wanted to sit and listen, but she was distracted by the crumbs on the floor.

Jesus noticed Martha's irritation, but He also understood Mary's heart to know Him. She was captivated with His words and longed to understand truth. Jesus seemed pleased that Mary didn't allow traditions or tasks or even her sister's expectations, to take her away from spending time with Him. He knew Martha needed to understand that her preoccupation with the household details wasn't as important as she thought. But in that moment, she was trapped in the social pressures of being the perfect hostess. Jesus unapologetically responded to Martha's outburst, "Martha, Martha, you are worried and troubled about many things. But one thing is needed, and Mary has chosen that good part, which will not be taken away from her" (Luke 10:41–42, NKJV). Clearly, the distracted Martha was missing the opportunity to simply be with Jesus—to spend quality time in His presence.

We can only imagine the thoughts and emotions of the two sisters in that moment. Did Martha understand what she was missing out on and the temporary value of those household distractions? Was Mary fully aware that there is only one thing worth being concerned about and she had discovered it? Whatever their thoughts, Jesus' message was clear. He wanted both sisters to know Him, to hear His heart, and to understand His words—that was the *best* choice they could make. In that moment, with Jesus as a guest in their home, spending time with Him was the most important thing. The crumbs and dust could wait.

From that moment, the time Mary spent listening to Jesus significantly impacted every day of her life—both the good days and the challenging ones. One of the most difficult days was when her brother, Lazarus, became extremely ill. Anyone who had seen Jesus heal the sick knew that just one touch from Him and Lazarus could recover. So, she and Martha sent an urgent message to Jesus about the dire situation. Jesus didn't come before the illness took Lazarus's life. Beneath a cloud of incredible sorrow, family and friends surrounded the grieving sisters. By the time Jesus finally reached Bethany, Lazarus had been in the tomb for four days. When Mary saw Jesus, she fell at His feet and said, "Lord, if you had been here, my brother would not have died" (John 11:32, ESV). It was a proclamation of faith—faith that had grown out of time spent at Jesus' feet.

Mary knew and loved Jesus, but His response revealed just how much Jesus knew and loved this precious family. Their sorrow moved Him to tears, and though Jesus knew everything was about to change, He felt their pain deeply.

What happened next was incredible: Jesus raised Lazarus from the dead! Tremendous joy and wonder filled Bethany that day! Sometime later Jesus was dining again at the home of His friends in Bethany. This time Mary was overcome with gratitude—the more she knew Jesus, the more she loved Him. She wanted to let Him know how much He meant to her. In an act of extravagant worship, she poured expensive ointment made from pure nard on His feet and wiped them with her hair. Others in the room didn't understand the extravagance, but Jesus knew exactly what was in her heart and He stopped them from questioning her motives.

To Mary, this was simply an act of worship. It reflected her knowledge of Jesus and her intense love for Him. However, her response of worship placed her in a moment that was much bigger than herself. Unknowingly, she was preparing Jesus for His burial. As He hung on the cross days later, laying down His life for her sins and ours, an aroma of nard lingered in the air.

Mary's life displays how clearly Jesus understands our longing to know Him—after all, He gives us the desire. His Spirit stirs our hearts to draw close to the One who created us and knows us best. Like Mary, when we seek Him we find ourselves caught up in moments we could never imagine. We discover He rewards those who diligently pursue a relationship with Him!

A Twenty-First Century Story

Many of the women who've made the greatest impact in my life are women who, like Mary of Bethany, have always made it a priority to spend time in the presence of Jesus. My mom, sisters, and grandmother are the first examples I encountered. The time they've spent with Him has significantly shaped who they are and how they interact with every person they meet. Each one has different gifts and personalities, but the one thing they have in common is knowing how to love!

Somehow, I knew from an early age that Jesus made the biggest impact in the lives of these women who loved me so well. Simply being with them created a desire in my own heart to be close to Jesus. While I don't remember a time when I didn't "know" Him, there was a moment when that knowing went from my head to my heart.

If I close my eyes, I can still smell the distinct odor of the old tabernacle and see where I was standing when I encountered God in a deep, personal way. I don't remember the sermon from that evening or who was leading the service, but I remember exactly what my ten-year-old heart experienced. *God is real! He loves me, and He wants me to know Him!* With as much maturity as my age allowed, I asked Jesus to forgive my sins, and I surrendered my heart and life to Him. I desperately wanted to know God.

I wish I could say from that moment until now I've consistently pushed aside all distractions and endeavored to know Him fully. The truth is, I'm too easily distracted. During the tumultuous teenage years, popularity, achievement, and *boys* were huge distractions! I made mistakes and pursued much less important things than knowing Christ. Thankfully, as a young adult, I began to recognize the distractions by counterfeits and focused instead on knowing, loving, and serving God. Yet even now, being a wife and mother, and having a full-time job . . . well . . . life can be distracting at times.

As I look back on my life, I believe God has always understood my desire to know Him. Though I've had many Martha-moments of being distracted by the temporal details of life, He has continued to reveal Himself to me. Thankfully, He sees and knows my heart! He patiently makes Himself known to me in so many ways. He shows His love for me through meaningful conversations with friends and family. He provides exactly what I need when I need it—revealing His provision and attention to the details of my life. His goodness surrounds me every day in the most ordinary ways—through the smell of fresh-cut flowers or the warmth of a Texas sunset that displays His extraordinary creativity and power.

Like Mary of Bethany, when I pull away from the temporal details and sit captivated at His feet, I experience deep insights from His Word. He speaks truth to my heart and reveals His character in ways that increase my faith, surround me with peace, and challenge me to be more like Him. When I choose to be aware of Him and listen to His voice, I become less self-focused.

Like Martha, it's easy to get distracted and confuse the insignificant with the important. The challenges in life create distracting thoughts. Some are major, *If I had the perfect job that fit my gifts and abilities I could be more effective,* or *I would be more content if I could spend more quality time with family and friends.* And some are minor, *If only my home were clean and tidy (especially my bedroom closet!) I would be at peace,* or *If I had a nicer outfit to wear I would feel more comfortable at this event.*

When temporal concerns override the eternal, I believe Jesus looks at me and says, "Kerry, you're worried and upset over the details of life and you're missing out on the one thing that's truly important. Make knowing Me your highest priority. Leave all the details of your life to Me. The longings you feel aren't about 'things' at all. I put those longings in your heart to create a desire to seek *Me*." Oh, friends, when I hear and respond to that gentle nudge, my desires shift from seeking Jesus for what He can do for me to simply knowing Him more. My life takes on new meaning, and I discover the fulfillment my heart longs for.

What about you, friend?

The prophet Jeremiah tells us that God will give us a heart to know Him. "I will give them a heart to know me, that I am the LORD" (Jeremiah 24:7, NKJV). The prophet goes on to say, "You will seek Me and find Me, when you search for Me with all your heart" (Jeremiah 29:13, NKJV). God promises that He will make Himself known to us! What an incredible truth! The God of the universe wants us to know Him. Oh, that we would refuse to be distracted by our temporal circumstances and surrender to the deepest desires of our hearts to know Him—*really* know Him.

Consider how God sees your heart to know Him:

- He has placed the desire to know Him deep within your heart.

- He is pleased when you take time to sit at His feet each day and discover more of His character.

- He wants you to be aware of His presence, even in your busiest moments.

- He promises to reveal Himself to you as you seek Him.

Dallas Willard said, "God loves us, and because he loves us he delights in us, focuses upon us, relates to us, and serves us. So, when we hear that a person is seeking God, it is evidence that God first loved him. . . . It's as if there were a sign on the door that leads to eternal life that said, 'Whosoever will may come.' So, you chose to walk through that door, and when you turned around to look back, you saw a sign above that door that said, 'You did not choose Me, but I chose you.' "[2] How precious is that!

THINGS TO CONSIDER

1. Where do you find yourself in this moment in your pursuit to know Jesus?

2. Are you distracted by the temporal details of your life?

3. How do you seize opportunities to pull away from outward expectations and simply be with Him, spending time in His Word and in prayer?

Scriptures to draw you close to God's heart

"I will give them a heart to know that I am the LORD,
and they shall be my people and I will be their God,
for they shall return to me with their whole heart."

~JEREMIAH 24:7, ESV

Oh, LORD, *you have searched me and known me!*

~PSALM 139:1, ESV

"But from there you will seek the LORD *your God and you*
will find him, if you search after him with all your heart
and with all your soul."

~DEUTERONOMY 4:29, ESV

And without faith it is impossible to please God,
because anyone who comes to him must believe that he
exists and that he rewards those who earnestly seek him.

~HEBREWS 11:6

Blessed are those who keep his testimonies, who seek him
with their whole heart.

~PSALM 119:2, ESV

The LORD *is good to those who wait for him, to the soul*
who seeks him.

~LAMENTATIONS 3:25, ESV

"You did not choose me, but I chose you and appointed you that you should go and bear fruit and that your fruit should abide, so that whatever you ask the Father in my name, he may give it to you."

~JOHN 15:16, ESV

Seek the Lord and his strength; seek his presence continually!

~1 CHRONICLES 16:11, ESV

The young lions suffer want and hunger; but those who seek the Lord lack no good thing.

~PSALM 34:10, ESV

APPLICATION/DISCUSSION QUESTIONS

1. Recount the moment you first felt drawn to know God.

2. What are some of the common distractions in your everyday life?

3. Read Luke 10:42 aloud. How does Jesus' response to Martha challenge us to realign our daily priorities?

4. How can we prioritize time "at Jesus' feet"?

5. Consider the characteristics of someone you know who spends time with Jesus.

Journal prompt

In Luke 10:42, Jesus said we should be concerned about only one thing: seeking to know Him. How can you adjust your thinking or your schedule to spend more time seeking to know Him more?

CHAPTER 3

Mary Magdalene—
The God Who Sees My Brokenness
John 20

KAY BURNETT

Jerusalem—During Jesus' Crucifixion and Resurrection

As darkness began to recede, the rose glow of dawn crept through the windows. Taking the spices and ointment they had prepared, the women lifted their lanterns high and hurried together to the tomb to prepare the body of Jesus. Mary led the way through the winding streets of Jerusalem, her lantern casting just enough light to guide her next step.

These three women, Mary, Joanna, and Susanna had become close friends since Jesus had healed each one—sickness, demonic bondage, and brokenness. Because of their newfound freedom, each had a passionate desire to follow Him and learn from Him. Mary was grateful she and a few others had the financial means to assist Jesus as He traveled throughout the region. She had left her home in Magdala to follow the Master who had set her radically free.

The initial desire of these women to help Jesus had turned into an incredible opportunity to serve Him—serve the One who had helped them in miraculous ways. If Jesus needed food on His journey through a village, they gathered the supplies and prepared a meal for Him. They washed and mended clothes, ran simple errands, and offered their support without hesitation, relishing the chance to serve Him in any way they could.

The twelve disciples had become like brothers to them as they all traveled along the way, staying close to Jesus. He continually taught them about God through private explanations of parables and through conversations along the roads from village to village. Somehow, Mary and the other women thought of themselves as disciples as well. They were fully convinced Jesus was the Messiah sent to set the Jews free. Their hearts were full of purpose and joy in serving Him.

Now, in the early morning hours after the Sabbath, the group of women walked quietly toward the tomb, each consumed by her own thoughts, her heart bearing the weight of grief over the loss of her Lord. Mary prayed silently for God's help to remain steadfast without Jesus and to find the courage to obey all He had taught them. As she breathed a quiet prayer for these women she had come to love, she lived again every heart-wrenching moment of the previous days. It seemed impossible to comprehend all that had happened.

In the hours before His arrest, Jesus had seemed somber and heavyhearted. His words warned them and reassured them at the same time. This had troubled Mary and the others. It was confusing. She had heard the disciples quietly discussing some of Jesus' statements. *Was He going to leave them? Why did He so frequently warn them about this?*

That fateful night, Jesus had taken the disciples with Him

to pray in the Garden of Gethsemane. The women, who stayed behind, had busied themselves with meal preparation and other practical needs. There was always much to do, especially as they were careful to maintain the Jewish traditions of their forefathers to honor the Sabbath and Jewish holy days. Little did they realize that a time of great sorrow and uncertainty began that night for all who followed Jesus.

Mary shuddered, shocked at Judas' unthinkable betrayal of the Messiah. One of His own trusted disciples had searched for Jesus in the Garden with a crowd of armed guards, priests, and Jewish leaders. Later, the other disciples told them that Judas had greeted Jesus with a kiss as he led the temple guards to arrest Him. Her heart and mind could never fathom what Judas had done.

The council of elders and chief priests put Jesus on trial for ridiculous, trumped-up charges. He suffered horrific beatings, whippings, and mockery throughout the night. Though the disciples had fled from the Garden, some sent word to the company of women and others about what was unfolding. They could do nothing but wait to hear how the trial progressed, every hour an agonizing eternity.

Word came early the next morning that Pilate had condemned Jesus to be crucified. The city turned upside down in utter frenzy as the news spread. Mary, along with the other women and some of Jesus' closest friends, followed closely as the crucifixion procession moved slowly to the hill of Golgotha.

Mary would never forget the chaos of the crowd. No longer were the people praising Jesus as they had just a few days ago. Instead, soldiers and religious leaders taunted Him, hurling insults and claiming He was nothing more than a criminal. Many in the crowd joined in, shouting unspeakable words of blasphemy at her beloved Teacher and Healer. Mary and the others pushed their way through the crowd, determined to be as near Him as possible.

They called to Him, weeping at the sight of His disfigured face. The soldiers and leaders had beat Him beyond recognition and crushed a crown of thorns onto His head. He fell repeatedly under the burden of the cross and from sheer exhaustion. Then the soldiers nailed Him to the cross, where He suffered agonizing pain, struggling to breathe.

As Mary watched the hideous crucifixion from the shadows, she hoped to get close enough to speak to Jesus, longing to help Him in some way and tell Him one more time how grateful she was for the freedom He had given her. The tight-knit band of women clung to each other as the crucifixion unfolded.

Mary and Salome wept and prayed alongside Jesus' mother and her sister. They heard Jesus cry out and saw Him breathe His last breath. Mary Magdalene felt her own breath forced from her with a wail from the depths of her being that pierced the air, punctuating that fateful moment.

These memories brought tears to her eyes as the women entered the garden near the tomb. Jesus had rescued her from utter, terrifying darkness, setting her free from seven demons that had tormented her for years. He had looked past her disheveled demonic appearance, His compassionate eyes piercing her heart—and He spoke love and hope to her tormented soul. With undeniable authority, Jesus commanded the demons to leave her. It was as if He could see the appalling life she had lived for years, controlled by the power of demons who had bound her with their vile presence, made her a despicable creature, and engulfed her in shame. Others had avoided her, fearful the demons would grab hold of them. She had been captive to this bondage of torment for many long years.

Then one glorious day Jesus had set her free. His words had come like a waterfall, washing the torment, pain, and shame out of her life forever. Instantly she was free! Free to think and speak clearly! Free to love and be loved! Free to be herself, not a shadowy, tormented being but a woman with a future and a hope.

At that moment she felt brand-new! The memories of that precious day filled her with joy and amazement. From that moment she had known Jesus was the Son of God, the Messiah—her Messiah! She vowed then and there to follow Him and serve Him in any way she could for the rest of her life. No matter what lay ahead, she resolved to serve Him by serving others, sharing what He had done for her until the day she died.

* * *

Morning dawned fully just as the women arrived at the tomb. They stopped abruptly, gripped by what they saw. Nothing was as they had expected. The stone was rolled away, and Jesus' body wasn't inside! *What had happened? Who had taken His body away in the night?* Mary hurried to tell the disciples this terrible news. Peter and John ran to the tomb and saw for themselves that Jesus' body was gone. They, too, had spent restless nights and days in turmoil, and finding the body gone from the tomb crushed their spirits. Who could have taken Jesus' body? Why would they take it? Confused, distraught, and uncertain what to do, they headed back to the house where they had all gathered. But Mary remained at the tomb, deeply troubled about the missing body of her Lord. Her last shred of composure broke, and she collapsed against the entrance to the tomb. Glancing inside one more time, she tried to wrap her mind around what might have happened.

Suddenly, two men appeared and spoke to her, "Woman, why are you weeping?" She tried to explain through her tears but struggled to make sense of it all. *Were these men or angels?* Turning, she thought she saw the gardener and asked him, "Please, sir, if you've taken His body away, please tell me where He is, so I can go to Him." Instead of a gardener, it was Jesus who stood before her. He quietly spoke her name, "Mary." Instantly she recognized His voice and realized who He was: her Healer, Teacher, Friend, Master, and Messiah! He wasn't dead, His body wasn't missing or stolen. He was standing before her, powerful, alive, and speaking her name! Jesus gently encouraged her, instructing her to go back and tell the disciples that He was risen. Happy to obey His every word, Mary ran, her heart full to bursting with praise, to share the great news with the disciples (John 20:1–17).

In the following days Mary experienced an incredible mix of emotions: joy, fear, hope, uncertainty. One thought filled her mind: *Jesus, her Savior, was alive and everything He had told His followers was true.* If God could set His Son free from the tomb, there was nothing He couldn't do in any life.

After Jesus was taken up into the clouds to return to His Father, Mary realized she faced the dawning of a brand-new day. Opportunity stretched out before her as she dreamed of pouring out her life in any way God might ask. She desperately, and joyfully, wanted to take as many people with her into eternity as she possibly could! Yes, this was a new day—a day filled with promise and purpose! Through her redeemed life, Jesus had demonstrated that no brokenness was too great for Him to heal. Her past would never define her life. She knew His glory resided in her, and His presence and truth would continue to lead her. From there, Mary stepped into a new ministry of sharing the good news of a Savior who rescues, heals, and sets free all who are bound.

A Twenty-First Century Story

Mary Magdalene's story is an incredibly affirming and encouraging story for all women, past and present. In New Testament times, Jesus consistently honored women by treating them as equal to men in value, honor, and worth. I believe God loves the way women serve Him with passion and depth when they devote their lives to Him. We clearly recognize the devotion of this group of women who served Jesus in His ministry. Mary and the other women lingered among the last at the cross—devoted to the end. They were also the first to go to the tomb. Mary Magdalene was the one to whom Christ intentionally chose to reveal Himself first as the risen Messiah. He honored her in an unbelievable way by choosing to appear to her, out of all the disciples. In the first century, society regarded women as so inferior to men that the testimony of a woman was not accepted in a court of law. Jesus boldly defied the culture of the times through His interactions with Mary, displaying God's love and respect for women.

Jesus' actions toward women throughout His time on Earth clearly communicate to us that women hold equal worth, merit, and
value in God's heart.

Some cultures today still view women as inferior to men. How
this must break God's heart. Having grown up in a household of
five sisters, I'm thankful to know that God sincerely values each of
us equally, without preferring one gender or race over the other.
From my childhood I've longed to feel significant, wanted, and
valued in God's eyes, as well as in the eyes of others. Galatians
3:26–28 tells us of the honor and love God holds for every person
in His family, regardless of gender, race, or status: "So in Christ
Jesus you are all children of God through faith, for all of you who
were baptized into Christ have clothed yourself with Christ. There
is neither Jew nor Gentile, neither slave nor free, nor is there male
and female, for you are all one in Christ Jesus." What a glorious
declaration to all who choose to follow Christ!

When I accepted Jesus as my Lord and Savior at the tender
age of eight, the Lord began a healing work in my life, especially
for the fears that gripped me. I was afraid of the dark, of danger,
of failure, and of tight spaces (I'm still working on this one!). I
was overwhelmed with the fear of rejection, betrayal, and abandonment. These fears followed me into adulthood, affecting my
marriage and plaguing me as a mom. I experienced ulcers, sleep-
lessness, nightmares, and hidden anxieties. In my early years as
an adult, life sometimes felt very messy and out of control.

But somewhere along the way, as I pressed into a deeper
relationship with God, healing and freedom flowed. I attended
small group Bible studies for women and learned others had
broken areas, too. Discipleship through training and teaching at

church helped me to develop the spiritual disciplines of reading my Bible daily, praying, and learning to listen to the voice of the Holy Spirit. I poured my life into serving in my church, which brought the gift of sweet friends to pray with me as I learned to trust others with my secret struggles. Today, I'm amazingly free of fear—a testimony to the power of God who still heals brokenness today!

Each one of us has areas in our life that are broken and stained by hurts and sin—whether our own sins or the sins of others. We each need the transforming power that comes only through devotion to our Savior and Healer, Jesus Christ. Praise be to God, He still heals and sets people free!

Though my friend Jessica's struggles were different than those of Mary Magdalene, Jessica also suffered a difficult and broken past. Raised in a home filled with alcoholism and abuse, her life was filled with constant fear and insecurity. To compensate for this she strived for perfection, hoping that if she excelled in school or in sports or any number of areas, her home life would be safer and happier. As a little girl, she often retreated to hiding places to escape the fights and abuse that ruled her home. After years of living in this broken family environment, Jessica suffered enormous anxieties and developed coping mechanisms. She was a strong survivor, coping with pain and abuse at home, while excelling as a student.

When she headed off to college on a full scholarship, Jessica thought she had escaped the pain and terror of her past. She looked forward to a brighter future. What she experienced, instead, was her own rapid descent into alcoholism and drug addiction. It wasn't long before she was living in a drug-filled house with people she hardly knew, spending her days doing whatever she had to do to continue getting high.

Yet she became desperate to escape this gut-wrenching lifestyle, so she decided to go to church. There she found authentic, loving friends who wanted to care for her and help her escape her destructive past and enter a promising, Christ-filled future. Jessica said yes to Jesus and has never turned back to her painful, broken past!

Today, Jessica gladly shares her story of how Jesus rescued her, knowing it will help others who are suffering and struggling with the pain of dysfunctional childhoods. The Lord has continually walked with her through healing into freedom. Jessica and her husband are church planters and pastors. With compassion and understanding they serve the many hurt and broken people God brings to their doorstep. Jessica radiates the light of Christ. Her joy in the Lord is tangible and infectious. She knows she will always need to lean hard on Him for strength and help in navigating the storms of life. Her authenticity and willingness to encourage others quickly endears her to everyone she meets. Her beautiful life demonstrates how the Lord still heals brokenness . . . of any kind.

What about you, friend?

Mary Magdalene is a beautiful example of a woman who found healing and redemption through the power of Jesus. Jessica's story is also one of healing from addiction and internal brokenness. Both women became powerful and effective ministers of the gospel! No bondage is too big for God to break. No captivity is too dark or complicated for the King of kings to replace with freedom! He sees your brokenness and He is undaunted.

Let's consider how God sees our brokenness:

- God sees the woman He created you to become, not merely who you are today.

- God isn't daunted by fear, addiction, or bondage of any kind because He's the perfect answer.

- God doesn't define us by our past.

- When we step into God's spiritual transformation, He invites us into new assignments.

- God can use our past brokenness for His glory and for the freedom of others.

I invite you to trust God to be the answer for any brokenness in your life. He can set you free from the bondage of substance abuse, pornography, fear and anxiety disorders, thought patterns that have kept your mind chained to the past, or the pain of a past abortion. He is your answer. Through the power of God's Word and the Holy Spirit, you can walk in freedom regardless what depths of brokenness you've known.

THINGS TO CONSIDER

1. Is there anything from your past that is a burden for you? Ask the Lord to set you free. Prayerfully consider asking a trusted advisor to walk with you through the process.

2. Are you gripped by fear? You don't have to live with crippling fear. Ask God to show you how to renew your mind through His Word. Ask a trusted friend to pray with you about it.

3. Lack of forgiveness can bind us to the past, keeping us broken. Ask the Holy Spirit to show you anyone you need to forgive. Ask Him for the power to walk in that forgiveness.

4. If you are struggling with addiction, ask the Lord for the strength to reach out for help. Consider finding a Scripture-based resource to work through with a trusted friend or mentor.

Scriptures to heal and fortify you

*Now the Lord is the Spirit, and where the Spirit
of the Lord is, there is freedom.*
~2 CORINTHIANS 3:17

*Therefore, if anyone is in Christ, the new creation has come:
The old has gone, the new is here!*
~2 CORINTHIANS 5:17

*He brought them out of darkness, the utter darkness,
and broke away their chains.*
~PSALM 107:14

He heals the brokenhearted and binds up their wounds.

~**PSALM 147:3**

[Jesus read this Scripture in the synagogue at Nazareth.]
*"The Spirit of the Lord is on me, because he has anointed me to
proclaim good news to the poor. He has sent me to proclaim freedom for the prisoners and recovery of sight for the blind, to set he
oppressed free, to proclaim the year of the Lord's favor."*

~**LUKE 4:18–19**

*"I, even I, am he who blots out your transgressions,
for my own sake, and remembers your sins no more."*

~**ISAIAH 43:25**

*"So do not fear, for I am with you; do not be dismayed,
for I am your God. I will strengthen you and help you;
I will uphold you with my righteous right hand."*

~**ISAIAH 41:10**

"I am the LORD *your God who takes hold of your right hand
and says to you, Do not fear; I will help you."*

~**ISAIAH 41:13**

Heal me, LORD*, and I will be healed; save me and I will be saved, for
you are the one I praise.*

~**JEREMIAH 17:14**

APPLICATION/DISCUSSION QUESTIONS

1. What are some common forms of brokenness many women experience today?

2. What tools or actions have you seen that help women succeed in the healing and transformation process?

3. How can the church help women reach their full potential even though they may have great brokenness in their lives?

4. How important is it to share our struggles with each other?

5. How can sharing our struggles give others the courage to reach for help?

Journal prompt

Prayerfully reflect over your life. Has God healed you from brokenness and brought you freedom? Thank Him and pour out your praise to Him in your journal. Ask the Holy Spirit to reveal to you any areas that are broken in your life today. Commit them to the Lord, asking Him to continue His healing work in your life.

CHAPTER 4

Deborah— The God Who Sees My Place in His Work

Judges 4–5

KERRY CLARENSAU

The Hill Country of Ephraim— In the Times of the Judges

After an exhausting day of settling disputes and praying with numerous people, Deborah walked slowly back to her home. It had been a long day; the line of people needing her wisdom seemed to stretch to the next town. Her heart was heavy from all the difficulties people had shared with her. As she walked along the dusty road, she prayed, *Oh, Lord, how I long for the hearts of Your people to turn back to You. Why do they blatantly ignore Your Law? If they would simply obey Your Law, they would experience the blessings You've promised to them. I believe with all my heart that if they would simply depend on You, oh God, You would deliver them from the oppression of Jabin. Lord, please help me to lead these people to return to You!*

With each passing day, Deborah grew more burdened for her people. The evil in Israel was rampant—everyone doing what seemed right in their own eyes, with no regard for God's Law. Their sin created a desperate situation. In many ways, the condition in the nation seemed hopeless. Years earlier Joshua had subdued their enemies, the Canaanites, but the Israelites had failed to drive all of them out from their land. Since God's people had turned their backs on Him, God had allowed Jabin, a Canaanite king, to oppress them. In fact, Jabin and his general Sisera had terrorized the Israelites for the past twenty years. With their nine hundred iron chariots, the Canaanites had a distinct military advantage over God's people. A victory over Israel's oppressor would require divine intervention!

As a prophet and judge, Deborah was able to discern the heart of God and share His Word with others. Many people looked to her to settle their disputes. With each conversation, Deborah communicated God's truth and the hope of deliverance. Over time, the hearts of the people began to stir. Those who knew the words of Moses understood that this oppression was a result of disobedience to God. They knew that repenting and turning back to Him was their only hope—He alone was their Deliverer. And thankfully, once again they were crying out to Him.

Early one morning, Deborah made her way to the palm tree the community referred to as the Palm of Deborah. That was where people came to hear God's Word through this powerful prophetess. Unlike most mornings, today she arrived before the crowd began to gather. She used these quiet moments to pray and intercede boldly on behalf of her people. At once she knew exactly what God was speaking—He told her to call for Barak from Naphtali and ask him to gather an army of ten thousand men. God was going to bring deliverance to His people! Deborah could hardly wait for someone to arrive, so she could send word for Barak to come at once.

Barak was aware of Deborah's ability to hear from God—her reputation was known throughout Israel. He was quick to respond to her request to meet with him. As Deborah told Barak what God was asking him to do, he asked her to consider the size and strength of Sisera's army. She noticed his courage diminish as he spoke of the Canaanite troops. Quite honestly, the odds were stacked against the Israelites in every way. She didn't respond to his question about Sisera's advantage, she simply reminded him that God was going to bring the victory. She could see Barak struggling to believe, and yet he said, "If you go with me, I will go; but if you don't go with me, I won't go" (4:8).

Without considering her own safety, Deborah immediately agreed to go into battle with him. She knew that Barak was the one to lead the army and God would go before them and fight the battle. Barak could have received his instructions directly from God, but because he lacked faith, he would share the victory with a woman.

Barak followed Deborah's instructions and gathered the men. Nervous conversations could be heard throughout the camp. One moment the men seemed certain God was orchestrating the battle plan and the next they feared certain defeat. They could be heard murmuring and whispering among themselves. "What are we doing?" "How many men will we lose in this battle?" "This is crazy!" "But, men, remember, Deborah seems confident that she heard from God." "We know she's a wise, strong leader." "Will we be the laughingstock of Jabin and his kingdom?" "Can we possibly find peace after twenty years of persecution?"

When Sisera heard the Israelites were gathering for battle, he laughed under his breath. "Well, this battle won't take long. I'll soon be back enjoying dinner with my family." With great precision, he summoned his nine hundred charioteers and gave them the battle plan. Little did he know the power of the Lord who would fight for Israel!

Deborah felt God's presence and leading as the Israelite army began to assemble. She knew God was about to deliver His people once again. On the day the Israelites were to march down from Mount Tabor, Deborah said to Barak, "Go! This is the day the LORD has given Sisera into your hands. Has not the LORD gone ahead of you?" (verse 14). Barak led the ten thousand men and the Lord sent a sudden rainstorm that left Sisera's chariots stuck in the mud (5:4–5). God gave every one of Sisera's troops into the hands of the Israelites!

Barak was about to seize the Canaanite general, but seeing the defeat of his armies, Sisera fled north on foot. Before Barak was able to capture him, Sisera arrived at the tent of a woman named Jael. It was customary for travelers to find protection in the hospitality of strangers. As this woman's husband was one of the Canaanites' allies, Sisera blindly trusted her kindness. But Jael was also part of God's plan of deliverance. She struck Sisera as he slept and killed him. When Barak arrived at her tent, he found the defeated general dead on the floor.

All that Deborah had prophesied came to pass. As a woman whose heart was set on God, she awakened people to the reality of God's providence. This incredible victory was the beginning of the defeat of the Canaanites. As a result, the Israelites experienced peace for forty years. Deborah—a prophet, a judge, and a fearless warrior—was also a poet. She penned a beautiful poem giving praise and glory to God for the deliverance of His people (Judges 5). She knew the victory belonged to the Lord. She called out and recognized the gifts and contributions of others. Deborah led the people to victory over their oppressors, and they experienced peace for forty years!

A Twenty-First Century Story

I met June Groom shortly after moving to Texas in 2015. She's unlike anyone I've ever known! June is a woman with vast experience, yet she's humble, unassuming, purposeful, and influential. Her life has impacted thousands of people in a unique and inspiring way.

Let me tell you a little about her background. She and her husband, Jerry, were married in 1964 and became youth pastors the following year at First Assembly of God in Kaufman, Texas. Jerry joined the United States Army in 1966 and was stationed in Frankfurt, Germany. When he left the army, they returned home to attend Bible college and later became lead pastors. In 1972 they adopted their daughter, Jeri Elizabeth. After pastoring for several years, they became World Missionaries to United States servicemen and women. Through a series of events, Jerry became a prison chaplain in 1981. From there he became the chief of chaplains for the Texas Department of Criminal Justice. This move brought about incredible change for June.

In 1982 she finished her degree in sociology, and the following year a door opened for her to serve as a correctional case manager at Coffield—a maximum security prison unit. Yes, you read that right! She went to work in a prison and spent twenty years serving the Texas Department of Criminal Justice. She also worked as an assistant regional director and ended her career as an assistant director of the Programs and Services Division. But the roles I found most surprising were her roles as senior warden of two prisons—one female and one male. *She was the senior warden in a male prison, ya'll!* (Just a little Texan twang coming out there.)

You might think that following a twenty-year career of working with individuals in the prison system, June would be ready to retire and enjoy some downtime. Instead, she became the executive director of Exodus Ministries in Dallas, Texas. This ministry is an intensive, comprehensive, residential discipleship program for previously incarcerated mothers reuniting with their children. Then in May 2013, an old nursing home was made available to June and she began renovations to open a home for women and children in crisis. She calls the ministry Forever Families, and it serves homeless mothers, mothers who are victims of domestic violence, women who've been caught up in sex trafficking, and mothers who were previously incarcerated. Her goal is to provide discipleship, counseling, and life skills to help these moms live productive lives with their children.

She and Jerry are also lead pastors of First Assembly of God in Kaufman, Texas—the same church where they served as youth pastors almost forty years earlier. This church embraces the women who are a part of Forever Families, providing them with a positive, supportive community.

Like the prophet Deborah, June is awakening women to the life God offers them. She is bringing rest and peace to their lives—one family at a time.

There's one more woman I'd like to tell you about, my Aunt Janice (pronounced Ja'-nees). She spent her working years as a butcher for A & P grocery stores in the Kansas City area, then took an early retirement more than thirty years ago to take care of her mother, my grandma. At the time of this writing, Aunt Janice is eighty-seven years old and lives in assisted living. But don't let the words "assisted living" fool you! Janice is an incredibly active woman for her age—she still drives, travels, cooks, paints, serves in her church, and actively cares for other individuals. She even corresponds regularly with a couple of young men from her church who are serving time in prison. She wants them to know they're valuable and prayed for! In the apartment complex where she lives, she knows everyone by name. Janice prays for people, leads people to the Lord, connects individuals to one another, bakes cakes for birthdays, takes people to doctor's appointments, and the list could go on and on.

My aunt has never had a formal position in her local church, but she continues to serve whenever and wherever she can. Here are a few of the things I know she has done *this* year: attended services every time the door is open, helped to plan the women's spring event, shared at Bible studies, cleaned out the church's industrial-size freezer after it was out for several days, and helped to make the food for a party of one hundred. If you were to talk to her, you would hear about the people she has helped, numerous miracles, and how *good* God is. However, you wouldn't hear about her aches and pains, though I'm sure she has many at the age of eighty-seven. In one way or another, Janice loves and serves every person she meets.

I want to be just like her when I grow up. She inspires everyone she meets to be a better person!

What about you, friend?

Think about all we can learn from the women we've just read about. Deborah teaches us so many lessons: she boldly did what God asked her to do, yet she didn't step beyond her assignment. She relied on Barak's gifts and his ability to lead an army. Barak played a secondary role to this great and gifted woman—he drew courage and inspiration from her presence. And another woman fulfilled her role in the victory as well—Jael! Together with Deborah's ability to hear from God, Barak's military skills, and Jael's courage, God used them to bring peace to the nation. Deborah celebrated Barak and Jael's contributions, yet gave all the glory to God in her song of victory. We must rely fully on God and at the same time celebrate the strengths of others.

June allows God to use her strengths and skills in a unique way. She has never backed away from intimidating places or shied away from unconventional assignments. Serving as a prison warden wasn't what she envisioned for her life when she married a pastor, but it was exactly what God had in mind for this beautiful, strong, faithful woman. In her seventies, she's still serving and making an impact in people's lives. While her position isn't visible to the masses, she's faithful to serve right where God has placed her.

And finally, my Aunt Janice, an eighty-seven-year-old widow who is loving God by looking beyond herself every moment and serving in simple, small ways every day. This is how she has lived her life—in her work in a grocery store meat department, in her neighborhood, in her church, and in her family.

Consider how God sees your role in His work:

- He created you and knows you intimately.

- He caused you to be born in this time and knows right where you are.

- You can trust Him to place you in the positions and situations where your gifts will benefit the body of Christ in the best way.

- All honorable work is God's work. Being a custodian, hairstylist, physician, judge, homemaker (or tent keeper), prison warden, or butcher are all part of God's restorative, redemptive work here on Earth.

- You don't have to do it all, only those things that are right in front of you.

- You can allow the opportunities to come to you and trust God to use you in ordinary and extraordinary ways.

- God wants to fight your battles and bring victory in your life; just be obedient to the open doors and promptings of the Holy Spirit.

We may mistakenly think we need to have a ministry position, a formal education, or a defined set of skills to work in the kingdom of God. The truth is, *God wants to use you right where you are with the strengths He has given you.* It may be in unconventional, even extraordinary ways, or it could be in simple, everyday ways.

THINGS TO CONSIDER

1. Are you currently discontent in the work you're doing?

2. How can you adjust your thinking about what you do?

3. How would your work change if you did every task as if you were working for God?

4. How would your interactions change if you encountered every person as if you were encountering Jesus Himself?

5. Are you seeking to hear His voice and His promptings in everything you do?

Scriptures to encourage your call

For you created my inmost being; you knit me together in my mother's womb. I praise you because I am fearfully and wonderfully made; your works are wonderful, I know that full well. My frame was not hidden from you when I was made in the secret place, when I was woven together in the depths of the earth. Your eyes saw my unformed body; all the days ordained for me were written in your book before one of them came to be.

~PSALM 139:13–16

Therefore, since we are surrounded by such a great cloud of witnesses, let us throw off everything that hinders and the sin that so easily entangles. And let us run with perseverance the race marked out for us.

~HEBREWS 12:1

For we are God's handiwork, created in Christ Jesus to do good works, which God prepared in advance for us to do.

~EPHESIANS 2:10

Do not think of yourself more highly than you ought, but rather think of yourself with sober judgment, in accordance with the faith God has distributed to each of you. For just as each of us has one body with many members, and these members do not all have the same function, so in Christ we, though many, form one body, and each member belongs to all the others. We have different gifts, according to the grace give to each of us. If your gift is prophesying, then prophesy in accordance with your faith; if it is serving, then serve; if it is teaching, then teach; if it is to encourage, then give encouragement; if it is giving, then give generously; if it is to lead, do it diligently; if it is to show mercy, do it cheerfully.

~ROMANS 12:3–8

The LORD will fulfill his purpose for me; your steadfast love, O LORD, endures forever. Do not forsake the work of your hands.

~PSALM 138:8, ESV

From him the whole body, joined and held together by every supporting ligament, grows and builds itself up in love, as each part does its work.

~EPHESIANS 4:16

Now to each one the manifestation of the Spirit is given for the common good.

~1 CORINTHIANS 12:7

But in fact God has placed the parts in the body, every one of them, just as he wanted them to be. If they were all one part, where would the body be? As it is, there are many parts, but one body.

~1 CORINTHIANS 12:18–20

From the day we heard, we have not ceased to pray for you, asking that you may be filled with the knowledge of his will in all spiritual wisdom and understanding, so as to walk in a manner worth of the Lord, fully pleasing to him: bearing fruit in every good work and increasing in the knowledge of God.

~COLOSSIANS 1:9–10, ESV

APPLICATION/DISCUSSION QUESTIONS

1. What stood out to you about the way Deborah fulfilled her role in God's work?

2. What about the way Jael fulfilled her role?

3. What about the way June Groom fulfills her role?

4. What about the way Kerry's Aunt Janice fulfills her role?

5. How are you encouraged to fulfill your role?

6. How can we minimize or misunderstand the importance of every person's role in God's work?

7. After reading this chapter, how are you encouraged to see your work and your personal interactions with everyone you meet?

Journal prompt

Is there something God is asking you to do? How do you want to respond to Him? Do you need to make an action plan to step into your role in His work?

5

Hannah—
The God Who Sees My Deepest Longings
1 Samuel 1–2

KAY BURNETT

Ramah and Shiloh—When Eli Was Priest

Oh, how this journey sorely tested Hannah. The long dusty walk to Shiloh required at least an entire day, but it wasn't the distance that tested her nor was it the hours of walking. The long walk and fresh air were a welcome distraction for her. She appreciated the chance to break up her daily routine. She looked forward to the time when she and her husband, Elkanah, and others in their family would gather to pray and worship the Lord. She especially looked forward to seeing her two cherished friends, Mahlah and Adah. Though they came from different villages, the friendship of the three women had developed through many years of meeting in Shiloh for the festivals every devout Jewish family observed.

Hannah smiled to think of her friends, but soon her thoughts returned to the sorrow she carried deep inside. She suffered from

the constant reminder that Peninnah, Elkanah's second wife—
her rival—had . . . *children*. Not just one or two, but many. The
sight of Peninnah's children walking together toward Shiloh, the
older ones helping the younger ones when they fell or wandered
off a bit, pierced Hannah's heart like a flaming arrow. Hearing
their chatter and watching Peninnah comfort the little ones
when they grew weary felt like salt poured into her wounded
heart. Everywhere she looked, Hannah saw women with babies
in their arms, children clinging to their skirts, bellies grown large
with precious life inside.

Over the years her dear friends Mahlah and Adah had birthed
children, their families adding a new member almost every year.
Even seeing how God had blessed these dear friends reminded
Hannah of her empty arms. A sigh escaped from her lips. Would
she never know the joy of nourishing her own child, cradling
him to her breast, and singing softly to lull him to sleep? Would
she never hear her own baby's giggle or enjoy priceless toddler
kisses? Sometimes the longing seemed to overwhelm her.

She couldn't fathom why she was childless. She had prayed
many years for a child but had no answer from God. Thankfully,
Elkanah loved her deeply. He had kept her as his only wife for
several years after they were married, hoping they would welcome children into their lives, but as time slipped by, he felt the
pressure to take another wife. He must have children. Society
dictated this, and the needs of life made children a necessary
help. He resigned himself to a second marriage, taking Peninnah
into their home.

At first, Peninnah was cordial to Hannah, but as soon as children began to arrive, Peninnah took every opportunity to flaunt

her motherhood in Hannah's face. It was painful for Peninnah to see that Elkanah loved Hannah more and preferred her. Peninnah knew her marriage was strictly for bearing children. Elkanah was a good man, a Levite, who was kind and devout. He took good care of Peninnah and all her children, but he loved Hannah with a fierce and ever-deepening love. Others noticed and commented, sometimes teasing Elkanah about his love for Hannah.

Hannah was grateful for Elkanah's devotion. She knew without question that he loved her faithfully and always would. She couldn't help but love him back with every fiber of her being, yet, she daily lived the reality of barrenness, her arms aching for the joy of cradling a baby—*her* baby. When the women in her village of Ramah gathered for washing or to fill their water jugs, some taunted her about her inability to conceive. Several were kind and sympathetic. The question continued to plague her, *Why had God closed her womb?*

The sun hung low in the western sky as they neared the city of Shiloh. The weight of Hannah's longing was more than she could bear as she and Peninnah worked to prepare a simple meal for the evening. Once in bed, Hannah lay her weary head down with silent prayers turning over in her heart as the tears flowed once again. How much longer could she live with this longing? How could she cope with the taunts, the loneliness, the disappointment? Elkanah saw her tears and mildly chastised her for the familiar grief. "Am I not enough for you? Don't I mean more to you than ten sons?" he had asked (see 1:8).

At the feast, Elkanah placed a heaping portion of food before Hannah, his way of publicly showing his favor, love, and honor, as Peninnah and others looked on. Unable to eat, Hannah pushed away from the table, Peninnah's mocking and provoking comments during the journey still ringing in her ears. Reaching a depth of despair beyond anything she had known before, Hannah quietly slipped away to the holy meeting place.

She entered the tabernacle, searching for a private place to pray. "Oh, mighty Lord of hosts," she prayed, "if only You would look down and see me. May Your eyes and Your heart take in my longing, aching soul! See my suffering and answer my cries. Remember me, O Lord, and may You not forget me! I'm Your servant. If You would only give me a son . . ." she paused. *Can I go through with it? Can I step into this desperate idea in my heart that I thought of during the journey to Shiloh?* Steadying herself, she remembered her lifelong desire for a child. She pushed past this last-minute fear and continued her prayer. "Holy One of Israel, if You will give me a son . . . I will return him to You, to serve You in the temple all his days. I will dedicate him as a Nazirite to You. If only You will remember me, O Lord, and fulfill my heart's cry."

Eli, the priest, noticed her silent weeping, her body swaying under the burden of grief, and lips uttering muted cries to the Lord. He immediately assumed she was drunk. Chastising her, he said, "Woman, put away your wine! Should you be drunk at a time like this?"

Hannah was shocked. "Never, my lord! I've had nothing to drink, but my heart is troubled, and I grieve to the depths of my soul. I've been pouring out my need before God, telling Him of my longings and sufferings."

Eli's face softened. "Go in peace, then. May God grant your request."

Hannah raised her head, "Oh, thank you, my lord! May I find

favor in your eyes!" Her heart flooded with a new sensation of joy! Could it be that the Lord Almighty had heard her cries and would honor the priest's declaration? Gradually, a deep peace washed away her despair. Without knowing how to explain it, Hannah felt assured that God would answer her prayer of so many years. She felt certain it would come to pass.

She returned to the family table and began to eat, her face glowing with peace and joy. Peninnah looked suspiciously at Hannah and busied herself with the needs of the children. Elkanah put his arm around Hannah, relieved to see she was no longer crying but was softly smiling. Something had quieted her soul. He offered his own silent praise to Yahweh for comforting his cherished wife.

The next few weeks flowed like a rapid current, carrying Hannah along as she kept busy with everyday chores, planning every detail of what she would do when God gave her the desire of her heart. Soon the entire village shared in her excitement as her pregnancy became apparent to all. Nothing Peninnah said could penetrate her joyful heart! All the hurtful words of the past melted away, her heart filled with the joy of answered prayer. A child was growing within her! A son, of that she was certain.

Hannah often cradled her growing belly, singing songs of worship to God and songs to her unborn son. He would be devoted to God from conception, offered to the Lord as a living sacrifice from the heart of his mother for lifelong service as a priest. She spoke to him in her womb as if he could understand everything she said. She promised him that he would be used by God for great things, holy things. She spoke destiny and holiness over his life, her hands lovingly pressed where she felt his movement.

Hannah spent every waking moment preparing for all she would need to care for this promised child. She gathered the items her mother and loved ones had given her years ago, gifts given in expectation of children in her early years of marriage. She cupped the soft blankets and swaddles in her work-calloused hands, breathing in the scent of lavender from the pouch she had stored with the baby's items. "His name must be Samuel, *'heard by God,'* " she softly, but firmly, stated to Elkanah.

Without question, God had heard the cries of her heart. In His great mercy, He gave her the promised son, a treasure beyond any earthly treasure. Baby Samuel arrived, and the entire village of Ramah turned out to offer blessings for Hannah's long-awaited child. The joy of his birth spread through the village. Elkanah's house filled with laughter and gifts for the newborn child. Hannah let the joy and festivities soak deep into her thirsty soul. How good and faithful was their God! She would never understand the years of lack and yearning; she only knew that for this child she had prayed, and God had finally, ultimately, said yes.

Several weeks passed, and once again it was time for their annual journey to Shiloh, but Hannah asked Elkanah to go without her. She explained that when Samuel was weaned, she would honor her vow to the Lord to consecrate him for a lifetime of service in the house of God. Elkanah agreed, amazed by Hannah's devotion, as she assured him that this was indeed God's plan.

Hannah prayerfully seized every moment to pour her heart and soul into little Samuel. She had much to teach him and so little time to accomplish it. She understood that she was called and appointed by God as Samuel's mother and earliest teacher.

She held him close, spoke her love for him continually, and challenged him never to waver in his devotion to God. She prayed for protection over his life for all his days. She pleaded with God for anointing and wisdom when Samuel would grow into a man, a priest for the people of Israel.

Difficult as it was, once her precious son was weaned, Hannah kept her vow to God. She took Samuel to Eli, the priest, and offered him to God for lifelong service. God caused the boy to thrive in the service of the temple, and the people came to revere and love him. The Word of God tells us, "Now the boy Samuel continued to grow both in stature and in favor with the Lord and also with man" (1 Samuel 2:26, ESV).

In the years following, Elkanah and Hannah, along with Peninnah and her children, made the annual journey to Shiloh. Every year Hannah made a new robe for Samuel, carefully bundling up her handmade gift for the journey, anticipating the time of sweet reunion with her ever-growing son. Eli encouraged Samuel's parents each year, praying God's blessing and provision of more children because of their sacrifice of Samuel. And God did just that, giving Hannah three more sons and two daughters.

A Twenty-First Century Story

Wow! Only our God could write a story so filled with longing and unexpected answers! He is still a God who cares about the longings of our hearts. He is still a God who can work amazing miracles to fulfill those precious longings. Infertility is a widespread problem for women, even today. Their stories are all individual with unique answers from God, but He is working in every situation.

Tina and her husband, Ken, had been married for eighteen years, eighteen long years filled with tears and the longing for children.[3] As a teenager, Tina lost one of her ovaries due to polycystic ovarian syndrome. Ten years into their marriage, Ken sensed the Lord speak to him that they would have a child. Both Tina and Ken clung to that promise, believing soon they would hold in their arms God's fulfillment of this promise. But eight years crept by and the promise still wasn't a reality.

Just before their eighteenth anniversary, Tina was in severe pain and asked Ken to pray for her. He put his hands on her abdomen to pray, and God spoke to him, "This is my creative process." Tina felt infuriated! *God's creative process? What was that supposed to mean?* The very next day, on their eighteenth wedding anniversary, Tina visited her doctor with the intention of scheduling a hysterectomy to end her twenty years of pain. Instead, the doctor discovered Tina was pregnant! Seven months later, Tina delivered a perfectly healthy little girl they named Rachelle. A year later, their son Jonathan was born. Only God can write such an unlikely and miraculous story!

Still, not everyone experiences this type of ending to their longtime prayers. Some, after years of failing to conceive, relinquish their prayer for biological children and embrace God's provision of children through adoption, rejoicing in His sovereign answer. Some women conceive but experience pregnancy loss, sometimes repeatedly, suffering untold heartbreak over losing a much hoped-for and prayed-for baby. It isn't unusual to hear of a couple enduring half a dozen miscarriages. God has multiple ways of answering our longings for children.

But there are other deep longings besides the desire for children. As women, we long for meaning, validation, acceptance, and love. Many times, God's ways confound and surprise us. The Word of God clearly reminds us of the immense difference between our human mind-set and God's mind-set: "For my thoughts are not your thoughts, neither are your ways my ways," declares the LORD. "For as the heavens are higher than the earth, so are my ways higher than your ways and my thoughts than your thoughts" (Isaiah 55:8–9, ESV).

If we allow it, the delay of an answer to a longing can lead us into disappointment, depression, and despair. All three of these take us down a path God never intended for us to travel. How can we live life well if we spend our days consumed by the fact that God hasn't brought fulfillment to our longing? How can it honor God if we spend our greatest energy and focus on what we *don't* have, rather than rejoicing in all we *do* have? When a mother cries out to God to rescue her unsaved adult children, God still calls her to live a joyful life in Him because He is enough. She can't control the circumstances brought by her children's choices; only God can accomplish spiritual things to draw them to Himself. She is called to do her part—pray, love, and model godliness. But what testimony does her life speak to her children and others if she lives in despair, unraveled and atrophied by her children's poor choices?

One young single mom attended our church and quickly committed her life to Christ. She was a successful professional in her field and had full custody of her son as his father was absent from their lives. She continually struggled over the difficulties they faced: financial needs, physical sickness, challenges with family members, school. Her response often defaulted to the three Ds of disappointment, depression, and despair.

Fortunately, several older women had taken her under their wings, encouraging her along the way, pointing her to the Word of God and to the presence of Jesus. At one particularly stressful point in her spiritual journey, she confided her latest challenge to a group of us at a small church event for women. "When will the drama end?" she wailed, throwing up her arms with emotion. One seasoned saint who was old enough to be her mother lovingly but firmly responded, "Never. This is normal life, sweetie. The challenges and trials never go away. We all face them. You'll always be hit by unexpected problems, issues, and needs. You just learn to rely on Jesus for the answers and to help you do the right things."

That'll preach! My young friend was longing for the day when she wouldn't have so many problems and struggles to deal with. That longing was distorting her view of the good life God had given and her many blessings. She completely forgot about the joy He offers supernaturally throughout every storm, whether brief or long-lasting. Some of her longings were good. She longed for a husband, someone to share life with and to help raise her son. She longed for ease in her financial needs. It's natural to long for these things, but we must place those longings in the safe and loving hands of God rather than making them idols on the thrones of our lives, controling our thoughts and shaping our daily lives.

We all have longings for good and godly things that require trust and help from God, knowing He alone can answer our cries.

We must trust that He is always at work. We can never presume to explain how and why God answers our prayers, especially when His answer doesn't produce the much-prayed-for result, but we can lean hard into a place of trusting Him.

What about you, friend?

The biblical story of Hannah has much to teach us today. She certainly serves as an example of pressing in close to God, faithfully asking for the answer to her greatest longing and seeing Him answer, even after so many years. She's a precious example to all of us who are mothers, to surrender our children to the Lord. Our children are not our possessions, but our treasures, entrusted to our care in an amazing partnership with God.

Hannah is also an example to us about other longings in life. Perhaps your dream has nothing to do with children. Instead, you may be praying for significance and fulfillment in your life's purpose. Your longing might be for an opportunity in ministry that God has spoken about to you but hasn't yet been fulfilled. Is your greatest longing to see a loved one come to know Christ?

Let's consider how God sees our longings:

- God cares about the dreams and longings of our hearts.

- God's timing is often different from ours, but we can place our trust in Him.

- God never wastes a season of loss, grief, or pain; instead, He uses it for great good.

- If you are a mom, God invites you to place your children fully in His care. He has their best life in store.

- If you make yourself available to Him, God will use you to help others through your own struggles and experiences.

Regardless of the obstacle or trial in your life, God is your answer. He's everything you need to see the breakthrough miracle or to face disappointments. He's everything you need to receive an answer only He can offer. Press in closer to Him and listen. Study His Word and ask Him for your heart's desire, believing that His plans are for your good and His answers are always framed by His undying love for you.

THINGS TO CONSIDER

1. What is the greatest longing in your life in this season?

2. Have you ever struggled with the thought that God isn't listening to you?

3. What lies might Satan be speaking about your situation that you can resist through Scripture?

4. Have you reached a place of surrender, or are you in a wrestling season with God?

5. What might God be saying to you about this longing?

Scriptures to encourage your call

All my longings lie open before you, Lord;
my sighing is not hidden from you.

~PSALM 38:9

"Blessed are you who hunger now, for you will be satisfied.
Blessed are you who weep now, for you will laugh."

~LUKE 6:21

"The LORD will guide you always; he will satisfy your needs in a
sun-scorched land and will strengthen your frame. You will be like
a well-watered garden, like a spring whose waters never fail."

~ISAIAH 58:11

The LORD is my strength and my shield;
my heart trusts in him, and he helps me.

~PSALM 28:7

Out of the depths I cry to you, LORD; Lord, hear my voice. Let your
ears be attentive to my cry for mercy. . . . I wait for the LORD,
my whole being waits, and in his word I put my hope.

~PSALM 130:1–2, 5

Jesus looked at them and said, "With man this is impossible,
but not with God; all things are possible with God."

~MARK 10:27

APPLICATION/DISCUSSION QUESTIONS

1. What are some commonly shared longings women have today?

2. What are some of the ways we might attempt to bring our own answers when God's answer is delayed?

3. What are some ways our physical and emotional health might suffer when we live our days in despair over disappointments?

4. What steps can women take to live a life of joy and fulfillment in Jesus during the challenging times of waiting for God's answers to their prayers?

5. What are some practical ways we can renew our minds and be victorious in the difficult seasons of life?

Journal prompt

Ask the Lord to help you know Him even more intimately through your seasons of longing. Consider writing a list of all the things you are grateful for during this journey of waiting. List your longings in your prayer journal, entrusting the answers into God's loving hands. Ask God to reveal to you any longing you may have turned into an idol in your life. Confess to Him your struggle and ask Him to help you surrender it to Him.

CHAPTER 6

Ruth—
The God Who Sees My Destiny
Ruth 1–4

KERRY CLARENSAU

Moab and Bethlehem—Before King David

Naomi sat in the sun that bright morning, tilting back her face to soak in its warmth. She closed her eyes and remembered exactly how the village looked when she and Elimelech left with their young boys, Mahlon and Chilion. The smells and sounds of Bethlehem flooded her memory, deepening the ache in her heart. If only she could return to the land she loved—where she had played as a child, where she had met her beloved husband, where her precious sons had been born.

The pain in her heart since her husband and sons had passed away was more than she could bear. Naomi was acutely aware of how her grief had hardened to bitterness. She even wanted to change her name to reflect her agony. *They should call me Mara since it means bitter!* She opened her eyes to consider the place she had called home these many years—this land that had taken the lives of her loved ones. Oh, how she hated the land of Moab! She didn't want to stay another day in this desolate place with people who worshipped pagan gods. After all, the only ones close to her now were her Moabite daughters-in-law, Ruth and Orpah, and they could return with her to Bethlehem.

In sheer determination, Naomi prepared for the long journey back to Bethlehem. Ruth and Orpah saw her resolve and barely said a word as they worked alongside her to organize what they could carry on the journey to Bethlehem.

It wasn't long until they found themselves miles outside of Moab. At the end of the exhausting first day, the three women stopped for the night. Naomi laid awake under the stars next to her beloved daughters-in-law, her heart filled with too many emotions to sleep. As the younger women slept, Naomi looked at these two who had lost their husbands and her heart broke for them. *Am I selfishly taking my daughters-in-law from their families and the land they know?* She wondered how people would receive them in Bethlehem. After all, Jewish law prohibited men from marrying women who worshipped pagan gods. *Would these young women be shunned?* Maybe she should go on alone.

The next morning, exhausted from the journey and a lack of rest, Naomi pleaded with the women to return to their mothers' homes. They could find new husbands and settle in their homeland. Orpah loved her mother-in-law, but she was relieved at the chance to return to the life she had always known. She wept as she kissed Naomi good-bye; but Naomi wasn't sure if Orpah's tears reflected sorrow or relief. They would miss one another, but even more than that, Orpah longed to be reunited with her family and friends.

Ruth's response was completely different. Even though her mother-in-law's sorrow made her a difficult person to be around,

Ruth sincerely wanted to stay with Naomi to honor the commitment she had made to Mahlon and his God. Her answer reflected her resolve, "'Do not urge me to leave you or to return from following you. For where you go I will go, and where you lodge I will lodge. Your people shall be my people, and your God my God. Where you die I will die, and there will I be buried. May the LORD do so to me and more also if anything but death parts me from you.' And when Naomi saw that she was determined to go with her, she said no more" (1:16–18, ESV).

Ruth's choice to follow Naomi reflected her love for her mother-in-law and a growing trust in the God they served. She was aware of the dangers they would face as widows. They had no male protection, no income, and no opportunity to pursue a better life. But Ruth was determined that Naomi would not suffer alone. After all, the only thing worse than suffering is suffering alone.

Thankfully, God protected them on their journey to Bethlehem. Once they arrived, Ruth seemed determined to do whatever was necessary to provide for her grieving mother-in-law. She soon learned how God's Law made provision for widows and was thankful for the opportunity to glean in the fields. Since Naomi understood the customs of this land, Ruth trusted her guidance every step of the way. Under the Law Ruth had the right as a widow to glean in any field, but it wasn't by chance that she chose to glean in the field of an unmarried nobleman named Boaz. God lovingly led her into the place of His provision and care by ordering her steps right into the oversight of this godly man.

It wasn't long before Boaz noticed Ruth's impeccable

character, diligent work, and willingness to serve her mother-in-law. In fact, the entire community noticed Ruth's love for Naomi. Her friends told Naomi that Ruth was better to her than seven sons! It was the greatest compliment anyone could receive in that patriarchal community where sons were preferred and the number seven was considered the number of completeness.

Little did Ruth know that she would become the wife of the kind landowner. She simply chose to love and serve Naomi as if she were serving God. Her humble devotion to Naomi placed her in the divine care and guidance of God, who guided her right into a place of love and provision. Boaz watched over Ruth from the moment he noticed her in his fields by inviting her to stay in the protection of his workers. He also allowed her to eat at his table and take extra portions home to Naomi. This provision extended beyond the time of the harvest. God put all the pieces together beautifully, so that Boaz and Ruth became husband and wife.

God gave Boaz and Ruth a son and they named him Obed, which means, "a servant who worships."[4] This name was a clear reflection of the couple's heart for God. They lived their lives as worship—serving fully and loving well those whom God put in their lives. This child brought incredible healing to Naomi's bitter heart. She loved this grandchild as her own and quickly discovered once again the redemptive power of love.

Ruth's decision to love and care for Naomi brought redemption to her personal loss, it brought healing to her mother-in-law's embittered heart, and it brought hope to a nation through her great-grandson David. But it doesn't stop there. You can find Ruth included in the genealogy of Christ. Ruth—a poor, widowed Gentile woman—is in the bloodline of Jesus!

A Twenty-First Century Story

I wish you could have a long lunch with my friend Beth Grant. She's such an inspiration! Everyone who knows her is positively impacted by her love for God and her commitment to serve Him by loving people in an extravagant way. Grab a cup of coffee or tea, find a comfy place to sit, and read her story as if you were getting to know a new friend.

From her early teens, Beth felt God's hand on her life and she surrendered to His call. Determined to go wherever He would lead her, she attended Central Bible College, where she met a young man named Brian who shared her call to full-time vocational ministry. After they were married, the couple eagerly served God in music and youth ministry. Beth thought she knew exactly what God's call and purpose looked like for her life. However, all that changed just four short years later, when at the age of twenty-five, Brian died in an accident. Everything Beth had envisioned for her future seemed to be buried with him.

Though Beth couldn't imagine the future without her husband, God brought godly people into her life who validated her call and provided open doors of ministry. On the day of Brian's funeral, his dad spoke one of the most powerful words of faith for her future. Through his own grief, he looked across the table at her and said, "Beth, I can't wait to see what God has in store for you." She was stunned because she couldn't imagine that God still had a plan and destiny for her—but Brian's grieving dad could.

Six weeks before Brian's death, he and Beth had met David Grant at a youth camp. The young couple immediately felt a bond with the young man planning to minister in India and the three promised to keep in touch. Shortly after the camp, David left for India. When he heard about Brian's death, David reached out to Beth just to see how she was doing. For a year they kept in touch by mail and phone. After a year of correspondence, David showed up and proposed to Beth. It was a difficult decision for her since she really didn't know David very well. They had never even been on a date because David had been ministering overseas. She had to hear from God!

Beth knew she and David were different in so many ways and this decision would require huge adjustments in her lifestyle. She would need to embrace unfamiliar cultures and travel to unknown places. But the more she prayed, the more she experienced God's peace. She felt deep in her heart that this relationship was special. After seeking God for several months, she left everything that was familiar to her to embrace life and ministry with David. She knew this man was a gift, a gift she had not pursued but one God had brought into her life.

Their first stop one week after they were married was India— at a large public meeting of ten thousand people. When David introduced Beth as his new bride, the crowd smiled and celebrated. When he said she had been a widow, an audible gasp arose from the crowd. People started talking among themselves, shocked that an eligible man of God would choose to marry a widow. According to their culture, David had married "damaged goods." In their minds, a widow's life ended with her husband's death—she would never remarry, her life would be over.

It was one of those defining, humbling moments as daughters of God when we must remember that our ultimate identity is not defined by culture, people's opinions, titles, positions, success, or humiliation in people's eyes. If people in India never accepted Beth or understood her marriage to David, she was determined to be at peace, knowing who God had created her to be. She quietly determined to walk with Him in obedience and in His presence without knowing what the new season looked like.

Thankfully, the culture of India is amenable, and brothers and sisters in the church were gracious and accepting. Over time, as Beth honored David and determined to practice living in God's presence, things changed. Many of the people who initially shunned her eventually became her greatest mentors. They imparted strong prophetic words in her life, encouraging her to be obedient to God's voice. They graciously took Beth under their wings and opened doors for a teaching and preaching ministry that she never imagined.

To realize God's destiny for her life, Beth had to step into a new season of her life with faith and humility. She had to seek God's heart and walk hand in hand with Him through the open doors. Embracing a season required that she release the past one—not rejecting or dishonoring it, but choosing not to dwell there. Beth bravely faced forward, giving herself to the new stirring of God's Spirit for her future.

Beth shared with me, "In every season of life, my heart has been to serve God—however and wherever He places me. If we're motivated to serve God and others with abandonment and humility, God and others make a place for us. We can miss God's destiny for us if we make conditions and demands on how or where we'll serve. The best servants in any culture are kept busy and are useful because they're available and faithful to serve their master and others. God has wonderfully unanticipated opportunities and joys for His daughters who delight in Him and embrace whatever He has for us.

"From the age of twenty-five, I learned to hold things, seasons, and positions lightly because of experiencing early loss. But through this, I learned how generous, good, and faithful God is. He continues to surprise me in this season of life—now I am Mimi to four beautiful grandchildren, a mother of two delightful daughters who are women of God, and a mature wife to a very special husband of forty-one years. God still opens doors to share with others and be a voice for His loving heart to those who are brokenhearted and dare not believe He could have a good destiny for them. I've experienced how He can make beauty out of ashes and sorrow."

Beth and David Grant have served the Lord faithfully for forty-one years, touching countless lives on several continents. After Brian's death, Beth had no way of knowing how God would choose to care for her, lead her, and use her life for His glory. She simply chose to trust Him completely, seek His heart in every decision, and lovingly serve the people He placed in her life. Like Ruth, Beth discovered God's plan for her life by embracing what was in front of her, not despising her circumstances, and humbly serving those in her path.

What about you, friend?

We learn so much from the life of Ruth. First, she grieved the deaths of her father-in-law, brother-in-law, and husband, but we don't see the bitterness in her heart that is described in Naomi's responses. It appears from the biblical account that Ruth grieved well and didn't allow her heart to despise the circumstances of her life. Second, she fully embraced the life right in front of her by choosing to go with her mother-in-law to Bethlehem. She didn't cling to Moab and the past; she set her gaze on the future and lived each day to the fullest. Third, she was determined to serve her mother-in-law by whatever means available. She chose to love Naomi and provide for her, even if it meant gleaning in the fields among the poor. What was the result? Faithful, hard-working Ruth walked right into God's abundant provision and destiny.

The same is true of my friend Beth. Despite the tremendous loss she experienced early in her life, she walked confidently with God into the future He had prepared for her. These two women are such an encouragement to us! Each of us experiences loss and unexpected, perhaps even unwanted, changes in life. A move to a new city, a devastating health diagnosis, the loss of a job, the sinful choices of a family member, or a change in our finances can create an incredible sense of loss accompanied with disappointment and discouragement. We may even find ourselves doubting if God sees us or has a future for us.

So, let's consider how God sees your destiny:

- Nothing that happens in your life takes God by surprise.

- He doesn't want you to allow grief or disappointment to harden into bitterness.

- He cries with you and understands completely the sorrow and discouragement you experience.

- However, He longs for you to embrace the life ahead of you and not cling to the past.

- The loss or change of plans can be a step to fulfilling your destiny in a beautiful way.

- He is working all things together for your good. And He still has good plans for your life.

- His greatest command is to love Him by loving those He has placed in your life. You will find His plans as you love and serve others.

THINGS TO CONSIDER

1. Where do you find yourself in this moment?

2. Have circumstances left you wondering if God can or will use your life?

3. Do you find yourself despising your current circumstances?

4. Are you clinging to the past or simply longing for different circumstances in the future?

5. How might you miss the opportunities right in front of you if you cling to the past or long for different circumstances?

6. What person has God placed in your life at this moment to love and serve?

7. What steps can you take to embrace the life right in front of you?

Scriptures to encourage your call

"I know the plans I have for you, declares the LORD, plans for welfare and not for evil, to give you a future and a hope."

~JEREMIAH 29:11, ESV

"He will wipe away every tear from their eyes, and death shall be no more, neither shall there be mourning, nor crying, nor pain anymore, for the former things have passed away." And he who was seated on the throne said, "Behold, I am making all things new."

~REVELATION 21:4–5, ESV

And we know that for those who love God all things work together
for good, for those who are called according to his purpose.

~ROMANS 8:28, ESV

The LORD is my shepherd; I shall not want. He makes me lie down
in green pastures. He leads me beside still waters. He restores my
soul. He leads me in paths of righteousness for his name's sake.
Even though I walk through the valley of the shadow of death, I
will fear no evil, for you are with me; your rod and your staff, they
comfort me. You prepare a table before me in the presence of my
enemies; you anoint my head with oil; my cup overflows. Surely
goodness and mercy shall follow me all the days of my life, and I
shall dwell in the house of the LORD forever.

~PSALM 23, ESV

But Joseph said to them, "Do not fear, for am I in the place of God?
As for you, you meant evil against me, but God meant it for good, to
bring it about that many people should be kept alive, as they are today."

~GENESIS 50:19–20, ESV

APPLICATION/DISCUSSION QUESTIONS

1. How can a sudden loss or even a major shift in our plans cause us to question God's goodness and His plans for our lives?

2. Discuss Naomi's responses to the losses in her life.

3. Discuss the ways Ruth embraced the future.

4. Discuss how Beth had to let go of her life with Brian to experience the life she has now.

5. What types of things can cause people to dwell in the past?

6. What is the danger of despising our circumstances?

7. How can we embrace the life that is right in front of us today?

8. Why do we find God's plans for our lives in loving and serving others?

9. How is our destiny found one day at a time? How does that challenge you to live each day?

Journal prompt

Ruth and Beth each embraced the life in front of them and didn't live in the past. Each woman also lovingly served the people God placed in her life. Is there a loss or a disappointment you need to let go of? What steps can you take to embrace the circumstances of your life today?

The Widow—
The God Who Sees Me Completely

Mark 12:41–44; Luke 12:1–3

KAY BURNETT

Jerusalem—During the Time of Christ

A light drizzle filled the air as Rivka stepped from her tiny, makeshift home. She stretched and willed her tired, stiff legs to get moving on this damp morning. Though her feet moved slowly, her heart was full of gratitude as she started the long walk to the temple. The closer she came to the center of Jerusalem, the more crowded the streets became. Rivka was aware of the way others looked at her. They saw poverty—a frail, poorly dressed woman. Her emaciated appearance caused some of them to feel sorry for her and others to turn away, but many people didn't even notice her. However, Rivka didn't feel poor or frail, and she certainly didn't mind that most people looked right past her.

Jehovah was her Source, and she had everything she needed. God had faithfully provided for every one of her needs from the moment her husband had died five years ago. No, she wasn't wealthy, in fact at times she wondered where her next meal would come from, but Rivka knew God and trusted Him with her whole heart! Day by day Jehovah met her needs in beautiful, surprising ways. His provision went beyond her physical needs—He saw her heart more clearly than anyone else. In her loneliest moments, she enjoyed secret conversations of the heart with her God. These encounters with Him miraculously replaced her sorrow with indescribable joy. Yes, she was truly rich, even if no one understood the "wealth" she experienced.

Today Rivka was on her way to the Court of Women to contribute to the treasury. She was so thankful to have something to give. It wasn't much, just two small coins, worth less than a penny, but it was all the money she had. Most people would be afraid to give away everything, but Rivka didn't hesitate. She believed that with or without the coins, God was going to provide for her in every way. He was a loving Father, and she was His grateful daughter. This was her way of helping with the needs of the temple and worshipping her God. After all, He was so, so good to her.

Rivka was unaware that Jesus was standing nearby watching the crowd of people give to the temple treasury and that He witnessed her extravagant act of worship. While she felt completely hidden in the crowd and unnoticed by most, Jesus saw her and immediately recognized a heart fully devoted to His Father. As He often did, Jesus called His disciples over for an impromptu teaching moment. Once they had gathered close enough to hear Him speak, He said, "Truly I tell you, this poor widow has put more into the treasury than all the others. They all gave out of their wealth; but she, out of her poverty, put in everything—all she had to live on" (Mark 12:43–44). This faith-filled woman had no way of knowing we would still be talking about her centuries later. Her simple act of worship revealed a heart that completely trusted and depended on God. She was able to say like the psalmist David, "The LORD is my shepherd, *I lack nothing*" (Psalm 23:1, emphasis added). May we all grow to the place where we fully rely on God for every moment of our journey. Only then can we experience the abundant life He offers. It isn't the type of abundance the world defines, which is dependent upon material wealth, physical health, and social status, but the abundance of the soul as we live in close relationship with our all-sufficient God. It is the richness the widow experienced, allowing her to give Him all she had.

How Does God See Me?

Not only do we learn about the inspiring trust of the impoverished woman, we also learn so much about Jesus and the way He sees us from what He said to His disciples:

- He sees us! Even when no one else does, Jesus really sees us!

- When He looks at us, He looks at our heart.

- He knows our weaknesses and loves us despite our frailties.

- He doesn't expect us to give what we don't have.

- He notices when we give Him all we have and we trust Him to take care of all the details of our lives—nothing pleases Him more.

Adored by the God Who Sees Me

He sees you and truly adores you, my friend!

He wants you to know He sees you completely—every struggle, every accomplishment, every fear, every joy, every weakness—and nothing diminishes His love for you. You are valuable to Him. Please don't compare yourself to anyone . . . not your sister or your coworker or the neighbor who seems to have it all together. He doesn't compare you to them, so you shouldn't either.

Only you can do what you were designed to do. Jesus wants you to love those He's given you to love—*your* parents, *your* siblings, *your* spouse, *your* children, extended family, and *your* friends. He wants you to do those tasks He puts in front of you *today,* and to serve Him in your own unique way. You may have the gift of hospitality, so give it all you've got and bless others with your unique gifts. Jesus will see! Maybe you enjoy serving behind the scenes. Even if no one notices what you do, Jesus does! You may be able to lead and influence others, so do it with all that is in you for His kingdom and His glory, because He is the One who has gifted you and is cheering you on.

How He longs for you to depend on Him for everything: for salvation from your sin, the healing of your broken heart, the fulfillment of your longing soul, the wisdom you need in the confusing moments and peace for the challenging ones, hope in despair, and grace when you've been wronged. You can't produce these results on your own, but the wonderful thing is, you don't have to! He sees you and longs to provide what you need moment by moment.

We pray you will grow more and more aware of His loving, watchful eye. He knows exactly where you are and what you feel. He knows what you need, and He longs to provide and care for you. You can fully depend on our faithful, all-powerful, eternal God. You can surrender every part of your heart to His safekeeping, and you can trust Him to lead you every step of the way until you see Him face-to-face. After all, He is the God who sees you completely and adores you extravagantly.

We pray for God's sweetest blessings and His richest presence to be in your life.

—Kay and Kerry

The eyes of the LORD are on those who fear him,
on those whose hope is in his unfailing love.
~Psalm 33:18

Notes

1. For additional information about the religious background of the Samaritan woman, see the *NIV Cultural Backgrounds Study Bible* (Grand Rapids: Zondervan, 2016), 1814–1916.

2. Dallas Willard, *Life Without Lack* (Nashville: Willard Family Trust, Nelson Books), 157.

3. https://news.ag.org/news/prayers-answered-18-years-into-marriage

4. Moisés Silva, *The Essential Bible Dictionary* (Grand Rapids: Zondervan, 2011), 44.

About the Authors

Kerry Clarensau is a speaker, mentor, author, and inspiring leader for women. She and her husband, Mike, were pastors of a culturally diverse church in Wichita, Kansas, prior to Kerry becoming the director of the national Women's Ministries Department of the Assemblies of God. Currently, she serves as the director of Women's Ministries for the North Texas District of the Assemblies of God.

Kerry is passionate about helping women apply God's Word to their lives in practical ways. She is the author of *Selah; A Beautiful Life; Redeemed; Love Revealed; The Love Revealed Challenge; Secrets;* and *Fully His.*

She and Mike live in the Dallas area. They have two sons, two beautiful daughters-in-law, and three precious granddaughters.

Kay Burnett has served more than twenty years in pastoral ministry with her husband, Jim, as well as eight years in district ministry to women. In 2016, she was appointed as the national Women's Ministries director for the Assemblies of God. She is passionate about the Word of God, spending time with Jesus, influencing anyone she can to pursue a deeper walk with Him, and devouring great books that make her heart ache for more. She is the author of *Voyage: Trusting Jesus in Uncharted Waters.*

Kay and Jim have been married for thirty-eight years and their greatest joy is their family—a son, Tyler (and his wife, Megan), and a daughter, Leandra (and her husband, Rusty), along with their five incredible grandkids: Brynna, Aurora, Kayla, Greyson, and Bexley.

For other books and devotionals
by these authors visit
MyHealthyChurch.com.

Kerry Clarensau

Kay Burnett